Better Homes and Gardens®

MICROWAVE VEGETABLES

Our seal assures you that every recipe in *Microwave Vegetables*
has been tested in the Better Homes and Gardens® Test Kitchen.
This means that each recipe is practical and reliable, and
meets our high standards of taste appeal.

BETTER HOMES AND GARDENS® BOOKS

Editor: Gerald M. Knox
Art Director: Ernest Shelton
Managing Editor: David A. Kirchner
Copy and Production Editors: James D. Blume, Marsha Jahns,
    Rosanne Weber Mattson, Mary Helen Schiltz

Food and Nutrition Editor: Nancy Byal
Department Head, Cook Books: Sharyl Heiken
Associate Department Heads: Sandra Granseth,
    Rosemary C. Hutchinson, Elizabeth Woolever
Senior Food Editors: Julia Malloy, Marcia Stanley, Joyce Trollope
Associate Food Editors: Linda Henry, Mary Major, Diana McMillen,
    Mary Jo Plutt, Maureen Powers, Martha Schiel,
    Linda F. Woodrum
Recipe Development Editor: Marion Viall
Test Kitchen Director: Sharon Stilwell
Test Kitchen Photo Studio Director: Janet Pittman
Test Kitchen Home Economists: Lynn Blanchard, Jean Brekke,
    Kay Cargill, Marilyn Cornelius, Jennifer Darling,
    Maryellyn Krantz, Lynelle Munn, Dianna Nolin, Marge Steenson

Associate Art Directors: Linda Ford Vermie, Neoma Alt West,
    Randall Yontz
Assistant Art Directors: Lynda Haupert, Harijs Priekulis,
    Tom Wegner
Senior Graphic Designers: Jack Murphy, Stan Sams,
    Darla Whipple-Frain
Graphic Designers: Mike Burns, Sally Cooper, Blake Welch,
    Brian Wignall, Kimberly Zarley

Vice President, Editorial Director: Doris Eby
Executive Director, Editorial Services: Duane L. Gregg

President, Book Group: Fred Stines
Director of Publishing: Robert B. Nelson
Vice President, Retail Marketing: Jamie Martin
Vice President, Direct Marketing: Arthur Heydendael

MICROWAVE VEGETABLES

Editor: Marcia Stanley
Copy and Production Editor: Rosanne Weber Mattson
Graphic Designer: Darla Whipple-Frain
Electronic Text Processor: Joyce Wasson
Contributing Photographers: Wm. Hopkins,
    M. Jensen Photography, Inc.
Food Stylists: Pat Jester, Maria Rolandelli
Contributing Illustrator: Chris Neubauer, Thomas Rosborough

On the front cover: Orange-Buttered Broccoli
(see recipe, page 31)

Every time I shop for produce, I'm surprised at the choices I have. What often catches my interest is an unusual vegetable or one that's out of season. Fresh asparagus in December is such a treat! And even better are summer's selections. Often on warm Saturday mornings you'll find me wandering through the farmer's market, loading my backpack with the season's best produce, at the best prices.

Fortunately for all of us, microwave ovens have revolutionized how we cook both fresh and frozen vegetables. Gone are the days of overdone, olive green blobs going by the alias of cooked vegetables. Now we can quickly and easily micro-cook vegetables so that they retain their bright colors, nutrients, and fresh flavors.

And that's what you'll find in this book—vegetables at their best. For example, look at Orange-Buttered Broccoli, which is pictured on the cover (recipe, page 31). It has only six ingredients and you can cook it in less than 10 minutes. That's not bad for such a spectacular side dish. Go ahead, look through this book. You'll find your old favorites as well as some new vegetable ideas, all of which can be made quickly and easily in your microwave. I think that you, too, will be surprised—and delighted—by your choices.

Marcia Stanley

BUYING GUIDE

BUYING GUIDE   10

Learn what to look for (and what to avoid) when buying fresh vegetables.

STEAMED VEGETABLES   23

Easy vegetable recipes that need few ingredients and can be ready for dinner in minutes.

VEGETABLE CASSEROLES   39

All-time favorite as well as new vegetable casseroles made in the microwave oven.

VEGETABLE SOUPS   51

Warm-you-up-quick soups that need just a sandwich to make a hearty meal.

STUFFED VEGETABLES 61

Hot vegetable shells mounded with savory vegetable fillings.

MASHED VEGETABLES 69

Includes everything from favorite mashed potatoes to elegant vegetable purees.

VEGETABLE COOKING CHART 75

A quick reference for micro-cooking vegetables.

INDEX 79

Bright-colored, fresh-flavored vegetables, full of nutrients. That's what your microwave oven has to offer—and that's what you'll find recipes for in this book. Looking for a quick side dish for dinner? How about Garlic-Buttered Cauliflower, page 29. Need an unusual appetizer or a sophisticated soup for a dinner party? Try Pea Pâté in Pods, page 72, or Gingered Soup with Cellophane Noodles, page 59. Here are recipes for familiar standbys and exciting new vegetable ideas. We think you'll appreciate how quickly you can cook them in your microwave oven—and you'll love how they taste.

Micro-Cooking Advice

Microwaves and vegetables are natural go-togethers, because micro-cooking is such an easy and quick way to cook vegetables. And best of all, micro-cooking preserves the vegetables' colors, flavors, and nutrients.

To ensure perfect results every time, review the information on these two pages before you begin your adventure with microwave vegetables.

Microwave Cookware

Micro-cook in any dish that allows microwaves to pass through it rather than be absorbed by it. If you're not sure which dishes are safe for micro-cooking, the following guidelines should help you.

A dish labeled as microwave-safe by the manufacturer should be fine for micro-cooking any of the recipes in this book.

When you don't know if a dish is microwave safe, consider the type of material from which it is made.

● White paper is fine for micro-cooking large amounts of foods, if the food is moist and the total cooking time is under 10 minutes. Never use paper to micro-cook for more than 10 minutes, or to cook very small amounts (¼ cup or less), because the paper could combust.

● Small amounts of metal are okay for micro-cooking foods in some ovens. Check your owner's manual to see if your oven is one in which you can use metal. Be sure to always have a metal container at least ⅔ full, and don't allow any metal to touch the sides or top of your microwave cavity.

● Glass or pottery dishes that are not labeled microwave-safe need to be tested before you use them in your microwave. Just pour ½ cup of cold water into a glass measure. Set it in the microwave, inside or beside the dish you wish to test. Micro-cook on 100% power (high) for 1 minute. If the water is warm but the dish remains cool, you can use the dish for micro-cooking. If the water is warm and the dish feels lukewarm, the dish is suitable for heating or reheating food, but probably not for micro-cooking food. If the water stays cool and the dish becomes hot, *do not* use the dish in the microwave.

Also, do not use a dish or plate that has gold or silver trim or markings. The metal in the trim or markings may blacken or overheat and crack the dish.

Covering Foods

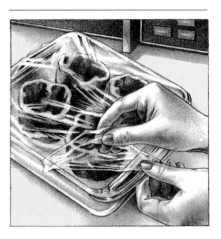

Unlike conventional cooking, microwave cooking is a moist method of cooking, which means that most foods will not dry out. But you'll still need to cover some micro-cooked foods to get them to cook faster. Covering holds the steam in, which causes the foods to cook faster.

When a recipe calls for a cover, use the lid designed to fit the dish you are cooking in. Or, cover the dish with clear plastic wrap, sealing the wrap to all sides of the dish *except* for one corner. The unsealed corner will act as a vent, allowing excess steam to escape rather than build up inside the dish. Keep the plastic wrap from touching the food, or use microwave-safe plastic wrap. If your microwave oven has a browning unit, don't use plastic wrap with the unit.

When your recipe says to loosely cover, place waxed paper or white paper towels atop the food. But don't leave paper towels in the microwave oven any longer than 10 minutes.

Rearranging Foods

Microwave ovens don't always cook evenly. That's why our recipes recommend rearranging or moving the food on the outside of the dish to the inside.

Stirring and Turning Foods

Stirring and turning is also used to help foods cook

Wattage of Your Microwave

Microwave ovens vary in wattage according to the manufacturer and model. All of the recipes in this book were tested in both high-wattage (600 to 750 watts) and low-wattage ovens (400 to 500 watts). Unless indicated otherwise, the timings given in the recipes are appropriate for either type of microwave.

But because individual ovens do differ, you may find that your timings vary slightly from the timings given in this book. The best rule of thumb for micro-cooking is to check the food at the end of the minimum time given in the recipe. Then add more time as it's needed to achieve desired doneness.

evenly. Microwave energy tends to penetrate the outside of foods first, so by stirring food you move the portion that was on the outside of the dish to the center. And turning the dish changes the location of the food in the oven, causing those foods in high energy areas to be moved to areas of lower energy.

Variable Power

Variable power means that a microwave has more than one power setting. Microwave ovens with variable power achieve power settings lower than 100% (such as 10%, 30%, 50%, and 70%) by cycling microwave energy on and off during the cooking time. Most newer ovens have from two to ten settings.

Many of the recipes in this book cook on 100% power, which means you should use the highest power setting

available on your microwave. When a recipe calls for 50% power (medium), use a

setting that is in the middle of the range of available power settings. If you only have two power settings on your oven (high and defrost), use defrost for those recipes that call for 50% power. A defrost setting is actually a little lower than 50% power, so it might take a minute or two longer to micro-cook foods on defrost.

VEGETABLE
BUYING GUIDE

With so many
varieties of fresh vegetables
available in both farmers'
markets and grocery stores,
it's hard to know what to
select. This buying
guide helps you know what
to look for in the produce
section, tells you when
a vegetable is in season,
explains what quality
of vegetable to shop for, and
outlines how to store
vegetables at home.

ARTICHOKES

Artichokes may seem like strange foods, but they've been eaten for years. They're available all year, but are most plentiful in the spring. Shop for bright green globes with tightly closed leaves. Avoid any with mottled leaves, spreading leaves, or shriveled cones.

Sometimes leaf edges darken in winter because of chill damage. This darkening, called winter kiss, does not hurt the quality of the artichoke. Store artichokes for up to 2 days in a cold, humid spot.

1 Artichokes
2 White Asparagus
3 Green Asparagus

ASPARAGUS

Both white and green asparagus are the young shoots of a fernlike lily. White asparagus is harvested while most of the stalk is below ground; green is harvested when the stalk is about 8 inches high. Select straight, fresh-appearing stalks with compact, pointed tips. The fatter spears are likely to be more tender than thinner ones. Store in the coldest part of your refrigerator, with bases wrapped in a damp paper towel. Grocers' supplies peak from April to June.

1 Green Beans 3 Broccoli 5 Brussels Sprouts
2 Beets 4 Lima Beans 6 Wax Beans

BEANS

Whether you're buying lima, wax, or green beans, look for plump beans with even color and fresh stem ends. The smaller beans in any variety are usually most tender. Avoid any wilt, rust, and shriveling on the bean or pod. Beans are available all year but are the most plentiful in the summer. If it's necessary, wrap and refrigerate beans for a day or two. But don't store shelled beans—remove beans from the pods just before you're going to use them.

BEETS

Beets are available all year around, but they are best when picked fresh anytime between late June and early October. If you can't get garden-fresh beets, look for those with crisp green leaves. The globes should be smooth, with dark red, unmarred skins. And for the finest flavor and texture, choose beets that are about

BROCCOLI

Broccoli is one of cabbage's incarnations—thick flower stalks with masses of tight buds that are harvested and eaten before they open. Although broccoli is available year-round, it's best and most plentiful from the fall through the spring. For the most flavor, look for broccoli stalks with tight green heads and no yellowish sprouting, rust, or wilt. Wrap and refrigerate broccoli for a few days, if necessary.

BRUSSELS SPROUTS

They look like tiny cabbages, but they're really brussels sprouts. Just like flowers, they tend to open if left on the shelf too long, so look for small, tightly closed heads with a bright green color. Avoid any sprouts with yellowing, wilt, rot, or insect damage. The best sprouts can be purchased from October into February. Before storing sprouts, remove any irregular, outer leaves. Loosely wrap the unwashed sprouts. You can keep them in the refrigerator for a day or two.

beets *(continued)*
the size of golf balls, because they become woody and lose sweetness as they grow larger. Check to see that the beets are not bruised or trimmed closer than 1 inch from the globe. You can refrigerate loosely wrapped beets for a few days.

13

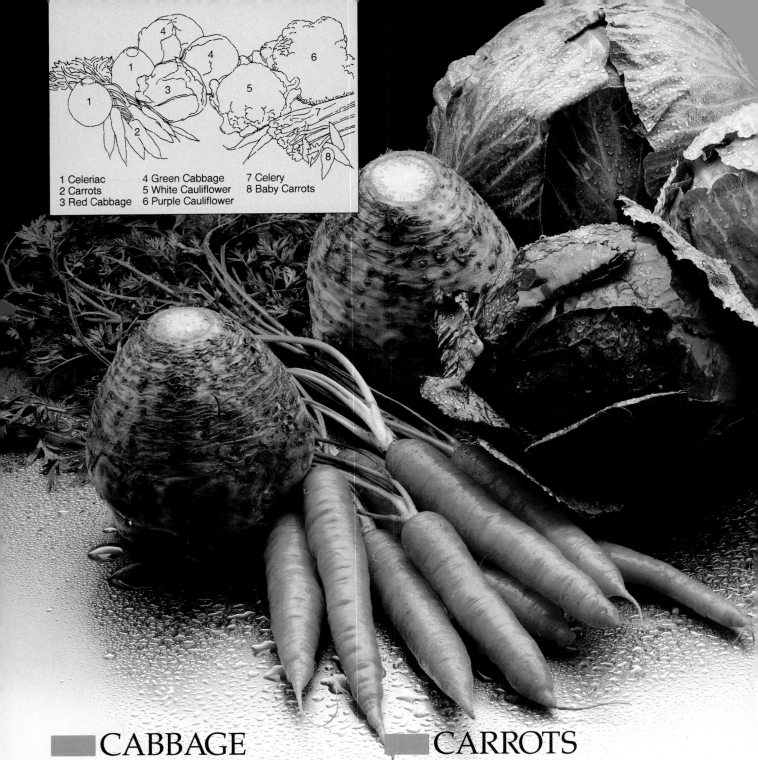

1 Celeriac 4 Green Cabbage 7 Celery
2 Carrots 5 White Cauliflower 8 Baby Carrots
3 Red Cabbage 6 Purple Cauliflower

CABBAGE

Very fresh cabbage has a delicate flavor and is likely to still have a few of its dark, loose outer leaves. But as cabbage ages, the outer leaves wilt and are trimmed away, leaving a small, pale head. Shop for solid, heavy, deep green or purple cabbage. There should be no wilt, rust, or limp leaves. The prime season is October through May, although you can usually find it throughout the year. To store cabbage, wrap loosely and refrigerate for one to two weeks.

CARROTS

The choicest carrots are medium-size, with the tops still on, because the condition of the tops tells you how fresh the carrots are. It's hard to judge freshness without the tops, but the best advice is to avoid cracked or brittle carrots with tiny white roots, or shriveled carrots. Baby carrots, available in many stores, can be either mature dwarf carrots or immature average ones. You can buy carrots all year-round. Store them in the refrigerator for one to two weeks.

CAULIFLOWER

Mark Twain once said "Cauliflower is nothing but cabbage with a college education." In a way, he was correct: cauliflower is cabbage that's trained to produce firm bunches of flowers. Most cauliflower is white or ivory, although occasionally you'll find purple or green. Look for solid, heavy, and unblemished heads. Avoid any that crumble easily. You can find cauliflower all year, but it's best in fall and winter. Store it loosely wrapped in the refrigerator for up to a week.

CELERY & CELERIAC

Celery, once an autumn vegetable, is now in plentiful supply all year long. Look for tight bunches with compact outer stalks. Never buy any that's brown or cracked. Celeriac is also available year-round, but is in short supply from May through September. Choose plump and heavy celeriac that's under 4 inches in diameter. Store both wrapped and refrigerated for several days.

15

1 Shitake Mushrooms   3 Eggplant   5 Cultivated Mushrooms
2 Enoki Mushrooms   4 Corn   6 Kohlrabi

CORN

Sweet corn is at its best when cooked and eaten within a few minutes of picking, because the natural sugars start converting to starch, and no modern technology can stop the process. When buying corn, look for fresh, green husks, fresh-looking silks (the ends are always dry), and cobs that are filled with plump, even rows of kernels. Avoid yellowed husks, shriveled kernels, and rot or worm blight. Use corn as soon as possible.

EGGPLANT

Eggplant seems to never be out of season. Purple eggplant is the most common and is available year-round. Occasionally, you'll find white, yellow, or gray eggplant in fall. Whatever shape or color you choose, look for a plump, glossy, heavy globe. Skip any eggplants with scarred, bruised, or dull surfaces. The cap should be fresh-looking. Wrap and refrigerate eggplant for a few days to store it.

KOHLRABI

Kohlrabi looks like a green tennis ball with a top of oval, dark green leaves. Although it's harvested in mid- to late summer, you'll find it in grocery stores in the fall. Look for small, uniform, well-rounded globes. Any kohlrabi larger than 3 inches in diameter is likely to have a woody texture. Also avoid cracked and split kohlrabi. Keep kohlrabi wrapped and refrigerated for two or three days if you need to store it.

MUSHROOMS

Mushrooms grow mysteriously, suddenly popping up where no growth had been before. Many varieties—shitake, white, and enoki—have been cultivated, making them available all year. Only nature can grow other types, such as morel, which makes them rare and expensive. When shopping for mushrooms, choose those that are firm and fresh looking. Avoid wilt, bruising, and rot. If necessary, store mushrooms, loosely wrapped, in the refrigerator for one to two days.

OKRA

Okra vary from bright
to pale green and from fuzzy to smooth. The
best tactic for buying okra is to handpick the
smallest from the batch, because larger pods
are more likely to be woody. Don't buy any
okra that is turning black or soft. It should be
plump and green. Look for the best okra from
June to September. To store okra, tightly
wrap and refrigerate for a day or two.

ONIONS

Onions come in many varieties—pearl, white,
red, and yellow, to name a few. But all are
available year-round, with the best quality
found in cool months. Choose firm, heavy
onions with papery dry skin and no scent.
A strong odor usually indicates a bruise
beneath the skin. Avoid sprouted onions,
because that's a sign of aging. Keep onions
up to a month in a cool, dry, dark, well-
ventilated place. Or, store them for a week,
loosely wrapped, at room temperature.

1 Peas
2 Snap Peas
3 Parsnips
4 Red Onions
5 Yellow Pearl Onions
6 White Pearl Onions
7 White Onions
8 Yellow Onions
9 Pea Pods
10 Green Onions
11 Okra

◼ PARSNIPS

Parsnips are cold-weather vegetables. They don't taste right until their starch has been converted to sugar, and that happens at near freezing temperatures. Today, modern technology has made them available all year, but they're neither plentiful nor at their best until fall and winter. Select parsnips as you would carrots—look for medium-size, plump, and fairly crisp vegetables. Avoid cracks, discoloration, and softness. Wrap parsnips and store them in the refrigerator a few days.

◼ PEAS

For good peas, shop at a farmers' market, so you can eat them soon after they have left the vine. Like sweet corn, peas have natural sugars that start converting to starch immediately upon picking. Pea pods and snap peas don't lose flavor as fast as regular peas. When buying peas or pea pods look for small, bright green, glossy pods and fresh stems. Avoid dull, faded, yellowish, or limp pods. Pea pods and snap peas are available all year, but spring is best for peas.

■ PEPPERS

Green and red peppers are common and in fairly good supply all year long. Other varieties—near-white, pale green, yellow, orange, and purple—are rarer and available in summer through fall. No matter what variety you're after, choose firm, glossy, bright-colored peppers. Avoid bruises, rotted spots, and shrivelled skins. Wrap green peppers and refrigerate them for several days. Other peppers can also be wrapped and refrigerated, but will keep only a day or two.

■ POTATOES

The many varieties of potatoes range from oblong to round and from creamy white to russet brown. In general, long, oval potatoes are mealy, making them good for baking or mashing. And round potatoes have firm, waxy interiors that are best for boiling. New potatoes are tiny, immature potatoes. Look for weighty potatoes that are firm, relatively clean, and smooth. Store them in a cool, dark place. If they begin to sprout, cut out the sprouts. Use potatoes as long as they're firm.

1 Butternut Squash 5 Acorn Squash 9 Chayote
2 Spinach 6 New Red Potatoes 10 Green Peppers
3 Zucchini 7 Spaghetti Squash 11 Red Peppers
4 Russet Potatoes 8 Red Potatoes

SPINACH

Spinach is in good supply all year long, with slightly lower quality and quantity during the hot months. Choose small leaves that are deep green and crisp. Don't buy any with wilt, yellowing leaves, rot, or bruises. Fresh spinach has an earthy green scent. A sour cabbage smell—or leaves with thick center veins—indicates that the spinach is old. Loosely wrap and refrigerate spinach for two to three days to store.

SQUASH

Squashes are classified as summer or winter, even though many are available all year. Summer squashes have soft shells and little seeds. Look for small summer squashes that are fresh, crisp, and unblemished. Store them loosely wrapped in the refrigerator for a few days. Winter squashes have hard, inedible shells and big seeds. Winter varieties ripen in the fall and can be stored in a cool, dry, dark place for up to a month. Look for those that are sturdy and heavy with a fairly glossy skin.

SWEET POTATOES

Sweet potatoes can vary from dark orange to almost white in color. They should be firm, unblemished, and not too misshapen. Small to medium ones are usually the sweetest and most tender, so avoid those that are overgrown. Store them at cool room temperature for a week.

TOMATOES

You'll find a big difference in color, texture, juiciness, and flavor between store-bought and vine-ripened tomatoes. If you can find a local source, buy vine-ripened tomatoes. In a store, choose tomatoes with the deepest red color and a delicate tomato fragrance. Store tomatoes for a day or two in the refrigerator.

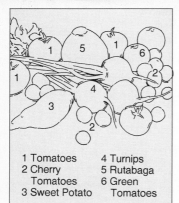

1 Tomatoes	4 Turnips
2 Cherry	5 Rutabaga
Tomatoes	6 Green
3 Sweet Potato	Tomatoes

■ TURNIPS & RUTABAGAS

Fall and winter are the easiest seasons to find turnips and rutabagas on the market, even though turnips are mildest and most tender in the spring. Choose roots that are plump and smooth. If there are any greens attached, they should be fresh. If the greens are trimmed, there should be no sprouting. Both turnips and rutabagas can be kept in the refrigerator for a week or two.

STEAMED
VEGETABLES

You won't need lots of ingredients or time to micro-cook flavor-packed vegetable side dishes. Just follow the simple recipes in this chapter and you'll discover the easy way to dress up everyday main dishes.

What Is Crisp-Tender?

Often a recipe tells you to cook vegetables till they are crisp-tender. But what is crisp-tender? It's the stage of doneness when the vegetables are cooked, but aren't yet soft or mushy.

Just like pasta that's cooked to the *al dente* stage, vegetables cooked till they are crisp-tender should be tender, but still slightly firm to the bite.

Toasting Nuts In Your Microwave Oven

You can quickly toast nuts in your microwave. Just put ½ cup of the desired shelled nuts in a 2-cup measure. Then cook, uncovered, on 100% power (high) about 3 minutes or till toasted, stirring after every minute. Be sure to always toast at least ½ cup of the desired nuts at a time so that you don't damage your microwave oven.

If your recipe calls for less than ½ cup of toasted nuts, store the extra nuts, tightly covered, in the refrigerator or freezer. This will keep them fresh-tasting for up to three months.

Savory Mushrooms

A 2-quart casserole might seem big, but it's needed to keep the mushroom liquid from foaming over the sides.

1 pound fresh mushrooms, halved
¼ cup chopped onion
1 tablespoon water
2 tablespoons butter *or* margarine
2 tablespoons dry sherry
1 tablespoon lime juice
1 teaspoon fines herbes, crushed
¼ teaspoon garlic salt

● In a 2-quart casserole combine mushrooms, onion, and water. Cook, covered, on 100% power (high) for 6 to 8 minutes or till mushrooms are tender, stirring twice. Drain well.

● Stir in butter or margarine, dry sherry, lime juice, fines herbes, and garlic salt. Cook, uncovered, on high for 1 to 1½ minutes or till heated through, stirring once. Serve with beef, pork, lamb, or poultry. Makes 4 servings.

Green Onions and Bacon

Serve this alongside or on top of broiled or barbecued meats.

24 green onions
4 slices bacon, cut into 1-inch pieces
¼ teaspoon dried marjoram, crushed
⅛ teaspoon pepper

● Bias-slice the white portions and 4 inches of the green portions of the green onions into 1-inch pieces. Set aside. Place bacon in a 1-quart casserole. Cover with white paper towels. Cook on 100% power (high) for 3 to 5 minutes or till crisp-cooked, stirring once. Drain bacon, reserving *1 tablespoon* of the drippings in the casserole.

● Cook onion, marjoram, and pepper in reserved bacon drippings, covered, on high for 3 to 5 minutes or till onion is tender, stirring once. Stir in bacon. Serve with beef, pork, lamb, or poultry. Makes 4 servings.

Eggplant and Tomato

1 small eggplant (about 1 pound)
1 tablespoon butter *or* margarine, cut up
2 medium tomatoes, seeded and chopped
½ teaspoon dried basil, crushed
¼ cup grated Parmesan cheese

● Wash the eggplant and cut off the cap. Peel the eggplant, if desired. Cut the eggplant, crosswise, into six slices. Place the eggplant slices in a 12x7½x2-inch baking dish. Dot with butter or margarine. Cover with vented clear plastic wrap. Cook on 100% power (high) for 5 to 7 minutes or till the eggplant is tender, turning the dish once.

● Toss the tomato and basil together. Top each slice of eggplant with some of the tomato mixture. Sprinkle each slice with some of the Parmesan cheese. Cook, uncovered, on high for 1 to 2 minutes or till heated through. Makes 6 servings.

Cumin Peppers and Onion

If you can't find a sweet red pepper, substitute a sweet yellow or green pepper.

½ of a medium green pepper, cut into strips
½ of a medium sweet red pepper, cut into strips
1 small onion, sliced and separated into rings
1 tablespoon butter *or* margarine
⅛ teaspoon ground cumin

● In a 1-quart casserole combine green pepper strips, red pepper strips, onion, butter or margarine, and cumin. Cook, covered, on 100% power (high) for 3 to 5 minutes or till the vegetables are crisp-tender, stirring once. Serve with beef, pork, lamb, or poultry. Makes 3 servings.

Peas and Walnuts

2 cups shelled peas *or* one 10-ounce package frozen peas
¼ cup chopped onion
1 tablespoon butter *or* margarine
1 teaspoon lemon juice
½ teaspoon dried dillweed
⅛ teaspoon salt
Dash pepper
¼ cup broken walnuts, toasted

● If using fresh peas, in a 1-quart casserole combine peas, onion, and 2 tablespoons *water*. Cook, covered, on 100% power (high) for 6 to 8 minutes or till peas are tender, stirring once. If using frozen peas, cook peas and onion according to the pea package microwave directions. Let the pea mixture stand, covered, while preparing the dill butter.

● For dill butter, in a 1-cup measure combine butter or margarine, lemon juice, dillweed, salt, and pepper. Cook, uncovered, on high for 30 to 40 seconds or till butter is melted. Drain the pea mixture. Toss the pea mixture with the dill butter and walnuts. Makes 4 servings.

Parmesan-Topped Tomato Slices

Richly topped with sour cream, mayonnaise, and Parmesan cheese.

2 large *or* 3 medium tomatoes, sliced ½ inch thick
¼ cup dairy sour cream
¼ cup mayonnaise *or* salad dressing
1 teaspoon lemon juice
¼ cup grated Parmesan cheese

● Place tomato slices in an 8x8x2-inch baking dish, overlapping slices slightly, if necessary. Stir together sour cream, mayonnaise or salad dressing, and lemon juice. Dollop atop tomato slices. Sprinkle with Parmesan cheese. Cook, uncovered, on 100% power (high) for 2½ to 4½ minutes or till heated through. Makes 4 servings.

Cumin Peppers and Onion

Hot Spinach-Bean Salad

Cook the dressing in a 2-quart casserole or bowl. You'll need the large size to toss the salad.

½ pound green beans *or* one
    9-ounce package frozen
    cut green beans
4 slices bacon, cut into
    1-inch pieces
1 small onion, sliced and
    separated into rings
2 tablespoons chopped
    pimiento
2 tablespoons vinegar
1 tablespoon sugar
⅛ teaspoon salt
2 cups torn spinach

● If using fresh green beans, remove the ends and strings. Break or cut beans into 1-inch pieces. In a 1-quart casserole cook the fresh beans and ¼ cup *water,* covered, on 100% power (high) for 6 to 8 minutes or till the beans are crisp-tender. If using frozen green beans, cook according to the package microwave directions. Let stand, covered, while preparing dressing.

● For dressing, place the bacon in a 2-quart casserole or bowl. Cover with white paper towels. Cook on high for 3 to 5 minutes or till the bacon is crisp-cooked, stirring once. Remove bacon with a slotted spoon and set aside. Cook the onion in the bacon drippings, covered, on high for 2 to 3 minutes or till the onion is tender. Stir in pimiento, vinegar, sugar, and salt.

● Drain the green beans. Stir the hot green beans into the dressing. Add the spinach and bacon, tossing to mix. Serve immediately. Makes 4 servings.

Toss the torn spinach and the cooked bacon with the hot bean-and-dressing mixture in a 2-quart casserole or bowl. The hot dressing, as well as the heat from the casserole, will help to warm the entire salad.

Garlic-Buttered Cauliflower

This can be ready for dinner in less than 10 minutes.

2 cups cauliflower flowerets
1 medium green pepper *or* sweet red pepper, cut into 1-inch squares
2 tablespoons water
1 tablespoon butter *or* margarine
2 cloves garlic, minced
⅛ teaspoon pepper
    Grated Parmesan cheese

● In a 1-quart casserole combine cauliflower, green or red pepper, and water. Cook, covered, on 100% power (high) for 5 to 7 minutes or till cauliflower is crisp-tender. Let stand, covered, while preparing the garlic butter.

● For the garlic butter, in a 1-cup measure combine butter or margarine, garlic, and pepper. Cook, uncovered, on high for 40 to 50 seconds or till butter is melted. Drain the cauliflower mixture. Toss garlic butter with the cauliflower mixture. Sprinkle with Parmesan cheese. Makes 4 servings.

Carrots and Pea Pods

Soy sauce and pea pods add an Oriental flair. Pictured on page 36.

2 medium carrots, bias sliced ¼ inch thick
2 tablespoons water
1 cup fresh pea pods *or* ½ of a 6-ounce package frozen pea pods
¼ teaspoon finely shredded orange peel
⅓ cup orange juice
1 teaspoon cornstarch
2 teaspoons soy sauce

● In a 1-quart casserole cook the carrots in the water, covered, on 100% power (high) for 2 to 3 minutes or till crisp-tender. Add the pea pods. Cook, covered, on high for 1 to 2 minutes or till the pea pods are crisp-tender. Let stand, covered, while preparing the orange sauce.

● For the orange sauce, in a 1-cup measure combine orange peel, orange juice, and cornstarch. Stir in soy sauce. Cook, uncovered, on high for 2 to 3 minutes or till thickened and bubbly, stirring every 30 seconds. Drain the carrot mixture. Gently toss orange sauce with carrot mixture. Cook, covered, on high for 30 seconds to 1 minute or till heated through. Makes 3 servings.

Sesame Cauliflower and Broccoli

Just a hint of lemon complements the vegetables.

1½ cups cauliflower flowerets
1½ cups broccoli flowerets
2 tablespoons water
2 tablespoons butter *or* margarine
1 teaspoon lemon juice
1 teaspoon sesame seed, toasted

● In a 1-quart casserole combine cauliflower, broccoli, and water. Cook, covered, on 100% power (high) for 4 to 6 minutes or till crisp-tender. Let the cauliflower-broccoli mixture stand, covered, while preparing the lemon butter.

● For the lemon butter, in a 1-cup measure combine butter or margarine and lemon juice. Cook, uncovered, on high for 30 to 40 seconds or till butter is melted. Stir in the toasted sesame seed. Drain the cauliflower-broccoli mixture. Toss lemon butter with the cauliflower-broccoli mixture. Makes 4 servings.

German-Style Potato
and Spinach Salad

German-Style Potato and Spinach Salad

¾ pound whole new potatoes
½ of a large red onion, sliced
    and separated into rings
¼ cup water
4 slices bacon, cut into
    1-inch pieces
¼ cup vinegar
1 teaspoon sugar
¼ teaspoon seasoned salt
¼ teaspoon celery seed
⅛ teaspoon pepper
3 cups torn spinach
1 hard-cooked egg, sliced

● Peel a strip around the center of each potato. Halve any large potatoes. In a 1½-quart casserole combine potatoes, onion, and water. Cook, covered, on 100% power (high) for 7 to 9 minutes or till the potatoes are tender, stirring once. Let stand, covered, while preparing dressing.

● For dressing, place the bacon in a 2-quart casserole. Cover with white paper towels. Cook on high for 3 to 5 minutes or till crisp-cooked, stirring once. Remove bacon with a slotted spoon; set aside. Stir vinegar, sugar, seasoned salt, celery seed, and pepper into the bacon drippings in the 2-quart casserole. Cook, covered, on high for 1 to 2 minutes or till boiling.

● Drain the potato mixture. Add to the dressing, then stir to coat. Cook, covered, on high for 1 to 2 minutes or till heated through. Add spinach, egg, and bacon; toss to coat. Serve immediately. Makes 4 servings.

Orange-Buttered Broccoli

Sweet peppers are often called bell peppers because of their shape. Pictured on the cover.

1 pound broccoli
½ of a medium sweet red
    pepper *or* sweet yellow
    pepper, cut into julienne
    strips
2 tablespoons water
2 tablespoons butter
    or margarine
1 tablespoon frozen orange
    juice concentrate
2 medium oranges, sliced
2 teaspoons sesame seed,
    toasted, *or* 2 tablespoons
    slivered almonds, toasted

● Cut the broccoli stalks lengthwise into uniform spears. In an 8x8x2-inch baking dish combine the broccoli, red or yellow pepper, and water. Cover with vented clear plastic wrap. Cook on 100% power (high) for 6 to 8 minutes or till the broccoli is crisp-tender, rearranging the broccoli mixture once. Let stand, covered, while preparing the orange butter.

● For the orange butter, in a 1-cup measure cook the butter or margarine and orange juice concentrate, uncovered, on high for 50 to 60 seconds or till the butter is melted. Drain the broccoli mixture. Arrange the orange slices and broccoli mixture on a serving platter. Drizzle orange butter over broccoli mixture. Sprinkle with sesame seed or almonds. Makes 6 servings.

Zucchini with Walnuts

Small zucchini (less than 7 inches long) are the most tender.

½ cup chopped onion
1 tablespoon water
2 cups zucchini sliced ¼ inch
    thick (about 8 ounces)
¼ cup broken walnuts, toasted
1 tablespoon butter
    or margarine
½ teaspoon lemon juice
½ teaspoon dried marjoram,
    crushed

● In a 1½-quart casserole cook the onion in water, covered, on 100% power (high) for 2 minutes. Stir in the zucchini and cook, covered, on high for 3 to 5 minutes or till the zucchini is crisp-tender, stirring once. Drain.

● Stir in the toasted walnuts, butter or margarine, and lemon juice. Sprinkle marjoram over vegetable mixture; toss to mix. Cook, covered, on high for 30 seconds to 1 minute or till heated through. Makes 4 servings.

Brussels Sprouts Parmesan

Parmesan cheese, garlic, and pepper add an Italian flavor to brussels sprouts.

2 cups brussels sprouts *or*
    one 10-ounce package
    frozen brussels sprouts
2 tablespoons butter
    or margarine
1 clove garlic, minced
⅛ teaspoon cracked whole
    black peppers
2 tablespoons grated
    Parmesan cheese

● Halve any large brussels sprouts. If using fresh brussels sprouts, in a 1-quart casserole combine brussels sprouts and 2 tablespoons *water.* Cook, covered, on 100% power (high) for 3 to 5 minutes or till tender. If using frozen brussels sprouts, cook according to the package microwave directions. Let stand, covered, while preparing the garlic butter.

● For the garlic butter, in a 1-cup measure cook butter or margarine, garlic, and peppercorns, uncovered, on high for 40 to 50 seconds or till butter is melted. Drain the brussels sprouts. Drizzle the garlic butter over the sprouts; toss to coat. Sprinkle with Parmesan cheese. Makes 4 servings.

Corn-on-the-Cob

Skip the boiling water. Just wrap the ears in waxed paper and pop them into your microwave for simple cooking. Pictured on page 7.

2 tablespoons butter *or*
    margarine, softened
½ teaspoon dried basil, dried
    dillweed, dried marjoram,
    dried oregano, dried sage,
    or dried thyme, crushed
⅛ to ¼ teaspoon salt (optional)
1, 2, *or* 4 fresh medium ears
    of corn

● Stir together softened butter or margarine; basil, dillweed, marjoram, oregano, sage, or thyme; and salt, if desired. Remove the husks from the corn. Scrub the corn with a stiff brush to remove the silks. Rinse.

● Wrap each ear of corn in waxed paper. Cook on 100% power (high) till tender, turning over once. (Allow 2 to 3 minutes for 1 ear, 5 to 6 minutes for 2 ears, or 9 to 11 minutes for 4 ears.) Serve hot corn with the butter mixture. Store any remaining butter mixture in the refrigerator. Makes 1, 2, or 4 servings.

Celery Amandine

Celery stays bright green when cooked in the microwave.

4 stalks celery, bias-sliced
   into 1-inch pieces (2 cups)
¼ cup finely chopped onion
¼ cup sliced almonds, toasted
1 tablespoon butter
   or margarine

● In a 1-quart casserole combine celery and onion. Cook, covered, on 100% power (high) for 6 to 8 minutes or till crisp-tender. Drain. Stir in the toasted almonds and butter or margarine till the butter is melted. Makes 4 servings.

Bias-slicing the celery
For an elegant-looking side dish, bias-slice the celery for Celery Amandine. With one hand, hold the celery on a cutting board or surface. With the other hand hold a sharp knife at a 45-degree angle to the cutting surface. Slice across the celery, making 1-inch-wide pieces.

Baby Carrots in Sauterne

If you can't find baby carrots, cut regular carrots into barrels like the ones shown at right.

1 tablespoon butter
   or margarine
¼ teaspoon dried tarragon,
   crushed
1 pound baby carrots
   or regular carrots cut
   into barrels
¼ cup sauterne wine
   or dry white wine
2 tablespoons snipped parsley

● In a 1½-quart casserole combine butter or margarine, tarragon, and ⅛ teaspoon *pepper.* Cook, uncovered, on 100% power (high) for 30 to 40 seconds or till the butter is melted. Stir the carrots into the butter mixture. Cook, covered, on high for 7 to 9 minutes or till the carrots are crisp-tender, stirring twice.

● Pour wine over carrots. Cook, covered, on high for 1 to 2 minutes or till heated through. Stir in the snipped parsley. Makes 6 servings.

Candied Acorn Squash

1 medium acorn squash
   (about 1 pound)
   Salt
   Pepper
¼ cup packed brown sugar
2 tablespoons butter
   or margarine
1 tablespoon water
⅛ teaspoon ground cinnamon

● Use a metal skewer to pierce squash in several places. Cook, uncovered, on 100% power (high) for 8 to 10 minutes or till tender. Let stand 5 minutes. Cut crosswise slices 1 inch thick; discard seeds and membranes. Place squash in an 8x8x2-inch baking dish; overlap if necessary. Season with salt and pepper.

● In a 2-cup measure combine remaining ingredients. Cook, uncovered, on high for 30 seconds to 1½ minutes or till boiling. Pour over squash. Cover squash with waxed paper. Cook on high for 2 to 3 minutes or till heated through. Makes 2 servings.

Orange Beets

1¼ pounds beets *or* one
   16-ounce can sliced beets
¼ cup packed brown sugar
1½ teaspoons cornstarch
½ teaspoon finely shredded
   orange peel
¼ cup orange juice
2 tablespoons finely chopped
   onion
1 tablespoon vinegar
2 teaspoons soy sauce
1 clove garlic, minced, *or*
   ⅛ teaspoon garlic powder
½ teaspoon grated gingerroot
   or ⅛ teaspoon ground
   ginger

● If using fresh beets, cut off all but 1 inch of the tops. Leave the roots on the beets. Place in a shallow baking dish. Add ½ cup *water.* Cover with vented clear plastic wrap. Cook on 100% power (high) for 18 to 22 minutes or till tender, turning the dish three times. Cool slightly. Slip off the skins and slice the beets. Set aside. If using canned beets, drain and set aside.

● In a 2-cup measure stir together the brown sugar and cornstarch. Stir in the orange peel, orange juice, onion, vinegar, soy sauce, garlic or garlic powder, and gingerroot or ground ginger. Cook, uncovered, on high for 2 to 3 minutes or till thickened and bubbly, stirring after every minute.

● In a 1-quart casserole stir together beets and orange juice mixture. Cook, covered, on high for 2 to 4 minutes or till heated through, stirring once. Makes 4 servings.

1 Cutting barrel shapes from carrots

If baby carrots are not available for Baby Carrots in Sauterne, you can make regular carrots look special by cutting them into barrel shapes. Start by cutting the carrots into 2-inch pieces. (If carrots are very thick at the ends, split the end pieces lengthwise.)
Then use a paring knife to carve around each carrot piece, smoothing the center and gradually tapering the ends so the pieces look like stubby barrels.

2 Testing the carrots for doneness

After cooking the carrots for 7 minutes, insert the tines of a fork into a few of them to check for doneness. If the carrots are crisp-tender, the fork will easily go in, but the carrots will still feel slightly firm. If it's hard to get the fork into the carrots, continue to cook them, but check for doneness every 30 seconds.

Carrots and Pea Pods
(see recipe, page 29)

Wax Beans with Tomatoes

Wax Beans with Tomatoes

Basil complements the fresh-tasting vegetable flavor.

¾ pound wax beans *or* green beans *or* one 9-ounce package frozen whole green beans
¼ cup chopped onion
2 slices bacon, cut into 1-inch pieces
1 medium tomato, seeded and chopped
½ teaspoon dried basil, crushed
⅛ teaspoon salt
Dash pepper

● If using fresh wax or green beans, remove the ends and strings. In a 1½-quart casserole cook fresh beans, onion, and ¼ cup *water,* covered, on 100% power (high) for 13 to 15 minutes or till crisp-tender. If using frozen beans, cook beans and onion according to the bean package microwave directions. Let beans stand, covered, while preparing tomato mixture.

● Place the bacon in a 1-quart casserole. Cover with white paper towels. Cook on high for 2 to 4 minutes or till the bacon is crisp-cooked, stirring once. Drain the bacon.

● Stir the tomato, basil, salt, and pepper into the bacon. Drain the beans. Place the beans in a serving dish. Arrange the tomato mixture atop the beans. Cook, covered, on high about 30 seconds or till heated through. Makes 4 servings.

Celeriac Alfredo

Enjoy the traditional flavors of Alfredo sauce (Parmesan cheese, basil, and wine) with the celerylike flavor of celeriac.

¼ cup sliced green onion
1 tablespoon butter *or* margarine
1 clove garlic, minced
½ teaspoon dried basil, crushed
⅛ teaspoon pepper
2 cups celeriac cut into julienne strips
1 medium carrot, thinly bias-sliced
¼ cup dry white wine
2 tablespoons water
½ teaspoon instant chicken bouillon granules
3 ounces spinach fettuccine *or* linguine, halved, cooked, and drained (about 1½ cups)
⅓ cup light cream
⅓ cup grated Parmesan cheese

● In a 1½-quart casserole combine the green onion, butter or margarine, garlic, basil, and pepper. Cook, covered, on 100% power (high) for 2 to 3 minutes or till the onion is tender. Stir in celeriac, carrot, wine, water, and bouillon granules. Cook, covered, on high for 5 to 8 minutes or till the vegetables are crisp-tender, stirring the mixture twice.

● Toss the vegetable mixture with the hot cooked fettuccine or linguine and light cream. Cook, covered, on high for 30 seconds to 1 minute or till the mixture is heated through. Sprinkle with the Parmesan cheese. Toss before serving. Makes 4 servings.

Asparagus with Lemon Sauce

For the freshest asparagus, choose spears with compact, closed tips.

¾ pound asparagus *or* one
    8-ounce package frozen
    asparagus spears
1 tablespoon butter
    or margarine
2 teaspoons all-purpose flour
⅛ teaspoon salt
    Dash pepper
½ cup milk
1 teaspoon snipped chives
¼ teaspoon finely shredded
    lemon peel

● If using fresh asparagus, wash the asparagus. Break off woody bases. In an 8x8x2-inch baking dish combine the fresh asparagus and 2 tablespoons *water.* Cover with vented clear plastic wrap. Cook on 100% power (high) for 4 to 6 minutes or till crisp-tender, turning the dish once. If using frozen asparagus, cook according to the package microwave directions. Let stand, covered, while preparing the sauce.

● For the sauce, in a 2-cup measure cook the butter or margarine, uncovered, on high for 30 to 40 seconds or till melted. Stir in the flour, salt, and pepper. Stir in the milk. Cook, uncovered, on high for 2 to 3 minutes or till thickened and bubbly, stirring after every minute. Stir in chives and lemon peel.

● Drain asparagus. Transfer asparagus to a serving platter. Drizzle sauce over asparagus. Cook, uncovered, on high for 30 seconds to 1 minute or till heated through. Makes 3 servings.

Oriental Vegetables

Bok choy is a dark green Chinese cabbage.

1½ cups sliced bok choy
6 green onions, bias-sliced
    into 1-inch pieces
1 tablespoon water
1 cup fresh pea pods *or*
    ½ of a 6-ounce package
    frozen pea pods
1 15-ounce can straw
    mushrooms, drained
2 tablespoons cold water
2 tablespoons dry sherry
2 tablespoons soy sauce
2 teaspoons sugar
1½ teaspoons cornstarch
    Dash pepper

● In a 1-quart casserole combine bok choy and green onion. Sprinkle with 1 tablespoon water. Cook, covered, on 100% power (high) for 2 to 3 minutes or till crisp-tender. Drain. Halve fresh or frozen pea pods crosswise. Stir pea pods and drained mushrooms into bok choy mixture. Let stand, covered, while preparing the sauce.

● For sauce, in a 2-cup measure stir together 2 tablespoons cold water, sherry, soy sauce, sugar, cornstarch, and pepper. Cook, uncovered, on high for 1 to 2 minutes or till thickened and bubbly, stirring every 30 seconds. Toss with vegetables. Cook, covered, on high for 1 to 2 minutes or till pea pods are crisp-tender, stirring twice. Makes 4 servings.

VEGETABLE
CASSEROLES

Make your all-time favorite vegetable casserole in the microwave oven! You no longer need hours for baking. Just toss the ingredients together and quickly micro-cook a casserole for dinner tonight.

Vegetable Casserole Tips

Baking Dishes and Casseroles

If your recipe calls for a baking dish, use a shallow glass dish that is square, round, or rectangular. If dish size is important, the recipe will specify. Otherwise, just use whatever dish you have. If a size is specified and you're not sure how big your dish is, measure across the top of the dish from the inside edges. Vented clear plastic wrap can serve as a cover for a baking dish.

A casserole is deeper than a baking dish, is usually round or oval-shaped, and often has a fitted lid. If you need to determine the volume of your casserole, measure the amount of water it holds when filled completely to the top. Remember that 4 cups of water equals 1 quart.

Simple Casserole Garnishes

You can easily make a vegetable casserole look great by adding a simple garnish. For example, try arranging olive slices, mushroom slices, green pepper rings, or pimiento strips on top. Or, accent the casserole with a few long, graceful fresh chives or green onions. And the tried-and-true idea of adding a sprig of fresh parsley brings interest to any casserole.

Cheesy Potato Bake

It takes just 20 minutes from start to finish!

3 medium potatoes, peeled
   and cut into ¼-inch-thick
   slices
½ cup water
1 tablespoon butter *or*
   margarine
1 clove garlic, minced
1 tablespoon all-purpose flour
   Dash pepper
½ cup milk
½ cup shredded American
   cheese (2 ounces)
½ of a 3-ounce can
   french-fried onions

● In a 1½-quart casserole combine the potatoes and water. Cook, covered, on 100% power (high) for 7 to 9 minutes or till the potatoes are just tender, stirring twice. Let stand, covered, while preparing the cheese sauce.

● For the cheese sauce, in a 2-cup measure cook butter or margarine and garlic, uncovered, on high for 30 to 40 seconds or till butter is melted. Stir in flour and pepper. Stir in milk. Cook, uncovered, on high for 1 to 2 minutes or till thickened and bubbly, stirring every 30 seconds. Stir in cheese till melted.

● Drain the potatoes. In the 1½-quart casserole gently toss together the potatoes and the cheese sauce. Top with the onions. Cook, uncovered, on high for 2 to 3 minutes or till heated through. Makes 4 servings.

Creamy Broccoli and Rice

Be sure the rice is quick-cooking, or it won't get done.

¼ cup quick-cooking rice
¼ cup water
2 cups broccoli flowerets
   or one 10-ounce package
   frozen cut broccoli
¼ cup chopped onion
1 tablespoon butter
   or margarine
1 teaspoon all-purpose flour
½ teaspoon finely shredded
   lemon peel
⅛ teaspoon pepper
⅓ cup milk
¾ cup shredded process Swiss
   cheese *or* American
   cheese (3 ounces)
2 tablespoons broken pecans

● In a 1-quart casserole combine the rice and water. Place the fresh or frozen broccoli atop the rice mixture. If using fresh broccoli, cook, covered, on 100% power (high) for 4 to 6 minutes or till the rice is tender. If using frozen broccoli, cook according to the broccoli package microwave directions. Let stand, covered, while preparing the cheese sauce.

● For the cheese sauce, in a 2-cup measure cook onion in butter or margarine, uncovered, on high for 1 to 2 minutes or till onion is tender. Stir in flour, lemon peel, and pepper. Stir in milk. Cook, uncovered, on high for 1 to 2 minutes or till thickened and bubbly, stirring every 30 seconds. Stir in cheese till melted.

● Drain the broccoli-rice mixture, if necessary. In the 1-quart casserole stir together the broccoli-rice mixture and cheese sauce. Cook, uncovered, on high for 1 to 2 minutes or till heated through. Sprinkle with broken pecans. Makes 4 servings.

Microwave Eggplant Parmigiana

This version takes less than half the time of conventionally baked Eggplant Parmigiana.

1 medium eggplant
(1 to 1¼ pounds)
¼ cup water
¼ cup chopped onion
¼ cup finely chopped celery
1 clove garlic, minced
2 tablespoons butter
or margarine
4 teaspoons all-purpose flour
1 14½-ounce can tomatoes,
cut up
⅓ cup tomato paste
¾ teaspoon dried oregano,
crushed
¼ teaspoon pepper
1 bay leaf
½ cup grated Parmesan cheese
6 ounces sliced mozzarella
cheese

● Peel the eggplant, if desired. Cut it into ½-inch-thick slices. In a 1-quart casserole combine the eggplant and water. Cook, covered, on 100% power (high) for 5 to 7 minutes or till the eggplant is tender. Drain. Set aside.

● In the 1-quart casserole combine onion, celery, garlic, and butter or margarine. Cook, covered, on high for 1 to 2 minutes or till vegetables are tender. Stir in flour. Stir in *undrained* tomatoes, tomato paste, oregano, pepper, and bay leaf. Cook, uncovered, on high for 4 to 6 minutes or till slightly thickened and bubbly, stirring every 2 minutes. Remove bay leaf.

● In a 10x6x2-inch baking dish layer *half* of the tomato mixture, the Parmesan cheese, and *half* of the mozzarella cheese. Top with eggplant, overlapping as necessary. Spoon on remaining tomato mixture. Cover with vented clear plastic wrap. Cook on high for 3 to 5 minutes or till heated through, turning the dish twice. Cut the remaining slices of mozzarella cheese into triangles. Top casserole with the cheese triangles. Let stand, covered, for 1 to 2 minutes or till cheese is slightly melted. If desired, garnish with a sprig of fresh oregano. Makes 8 servings.

Easy Green Bean Casserole

This microwave version of the classic Green Bean Casserole makes four servings—just right for today's smaller families.

1 9-ounce package frozen cut
green beans
1 7½-ounce can
semi-condensed cream
of mushroom soup
¼ cup dairy sour cream
1 tablespoon chopped
pimiento
¼ of a 3-ounce can
french-fried onions

● In a 1-quart casserole cook the green beans according to the package microwave directions. Drain the beans.

● In the 1-quart casserole stir together mushroom soup, sour cream, and pimiento. Stir in beans. Cook, uncovered, on 100% power (high) for 4 to 6 minutes or till bubbly, stirring twice. Sprinkle french-fried onions atop. Makes 4 servings.

Microwave Eggplant Parmigiana

Spicy Squash Bake

Spicy Squash Bake

Check your grocer's Mexican section for bottled salsa.

1 pound of a banana squash
　or butternut squash,
　peeled and cut into
　¾-inch cubes
2 tablespoons water
¼ cup finely chopped onion
1 clove garlic, minced
1 tablespoon butter *or*
　margarine
½ cup salsa
½ cup shredded cheddar
　cheese (2 ounces)
⅛ teaspoon pepper

● In a 1½-quart casserole combine the squash cubes and water. Cook, covered, on 100% power (high) for 6 to 8 minutes or till tender, stirring once. Drain. In the 1-quart casserole cook the onion and garlic in butter or margarine, uncovered, on high for 1 to 2 minutes or till the onion is tender.

● Stir the salsa, *half* of the cheese, and the pepper into the onion mixture. Gently fold in the squash. Cook, uncovered, on high for 2 to 3 minutes or till heated through. Top with the remaining cheese. Let stand, covered, for 1 to 2 minutes or till cheese is melted. Makes 4 servings.

Harvest Vegetable Bake

You can get these fresh vegetables during the fall and winter.

1 cup shredded carrot
½ cup shredded rutabaga
¼ cup shredded sweet potato
2 tablespoons chopped onion
1 tablespoon water
1½ cups cooked rice
¾ cup shredded Monterey
　Jack cheese (3 ounces)
¼ cup milk
¼ teaspoon salt
¼ teaspoon lemon pepper
　Dash ground nutmeg
¼ cup shredded Monterey
　Jack cheese (1 ounce)
　Green onion (optional)

● In a 1-quart casserole combine carrot, rutabaga, sweet potato, onion, and water. Cook, covered, on 100% power (high) for 2 to 4 minutes or just till vegetables are tender, stirring once.

● Stir in cooked rice, ¾ cup cheese, milk, salt, lemon pepper, and nutmeg. Cook, uncovered, on high for 4 to 6 minutes or till heated through, stirring once. Sprinkle the ¼ cup cheese atop. Let stand, covered, for 2 to 3 minutes or till the cheese is melted. Garnish with green onion, if desired. Makes 4 servings.

Fast Baked Beans

Mix canned kidney beans with canned pork and beans for a fast fix-up.

3 slices bacon, cut into 1-inch pieces
1 16-ounce can pork and beans in tomato sauce
1 8-ounce can red kidney beans, drained
¼ cup packed brown sugar
¼ cup chopped onion *or* ⅛ teaspoon onion powder
¼ cup catsup
1 tablespoon Worcestershire sauce
1 teaspoon prepared mustard

● Place bacon in a 1-quart casserole. Cover with white paper towels. Cook bacon on 100% power (high) for 3 to 5 minutes or till crisp-cooked, stirring once. Drain off fat. Set bacon aside.

● In the 1-quart casserole stir together the *undrained* pork and beans, drained kidney beans, brown sugar, onion or onion powder, catsup, Worcestershire sauce, and mustard. Cook, covered, on high for 6 to 8 minutes or till heated through, stirring twice. Sprinkle bacon atop. Makes 5 servings.

Molasses Beans

It takes less than 15 minutes to bring these tasty beans to your dinner table.

½ cup chopped onion
2 slices bacon, cut into 1-inch pieces
1 15-ounce can great northern beans, drained
3 tablespoons light molasses
2 tablespoons brown sugar
¾ teaspoon dry mustard

● In a 1-quart casserole combine the onion and bacon. Cover with white paper towels. Cook on 100% power (high) for 4 to 6 minutes or till the onion is tender and the bacon is crisp-cooked, stirring once. Drain off fat.

● Stir in the drained beans, molasses, brown sugar, and dry mustard. Cook, covered, on high for 3 to 5 minutes or till bubbly, stirring once. Makes 4 servings.

Easy Vegetable-Rice Bake

2 cups loose-pack frozen mixed broccoli, carrot, and cauliflower
2 tablespoons water
1 cup cooked rice
2 ounces American cheese, cut up (½ cup)
¼ cup milk
½ cup canned French-fried onions *or* toasted nuts

● In a 1-quart casserole cook the mixed vegetables and water on 100% power (high) for 3 to 5 minutes or till tender; drain. Stir in the rice, American cheese, and milk. Cook, covered, on high for 2 to 4 minutes or till heated through, stirring twice. Sprinkle with onions or nuts. Makes 4 servings.

Squash-Corn Casserole

1 1-pound butternut squash
2 tablespoons water
½ cup chopped onion
½ cup chopped green pepper
2 tablespoons butter *or* margarine
1 17-ounce can cream-style corn
1 cup coarsely crushed rich round crackers (21 crackers)
½ cup shredded American cheese (2 ounces)
2 tablespoons chopped pimiento
¼ cup chopped pecans *or* walnuts

● Halve the squash lengthwise and crosswise. Scoop out the seeds and membrane. In a 1½-quart casserole place squash pieces. Add water. Cook, covered, on 100% power (high) for 9 to 11 minutes or till squash is tender, rearranging squash once. Drain the squash and casserole. Scoop out pulp. Mash the pulp.

● In the 1½-quart casserole cook the onion and green pepper in butter or margarine, covered, on high for 2 to 3 minutes or till onion and green pepper are just tender. Stir in mashed squash, corn, crushed crackers, cheese, and pimiento.

● Cook the squash mixture, covered, on high for 4½ to 6½ minutes or till heated through, stirring once. Sprinkle the chopped nuts atop the casserole. Makes 6 servings.

Instead of covering the entire surface with chopped pecans or walnuts, try sprinkling them around the edge for a different presentation.

Custard-in-Squash Pie

Custard-in-Squash Pie

This savory side dish works only in a 600- to 700-watt microwave oven. If you're not sure of your oven's wattage, check the owner's manual.

2 small green zucchini, yellow zucchini, *or* yellow summer squash, cut into ¼-inch-thick slices (2 cups)
½ cup sliced green onion
2 tablespoons water
2 cups cooked rice
1 5-ounce can (⅔ cup) evaporated milk
2 slightly beaten eggs
1 cup shredded Monterey Jack cheese with jalapeño peppers *or* Monterey Jack cheese (4 ounces)
¼ teaspoon salt
1 small tomato, chopped
Sliced green onion (optional)

● In a 1-quart casserole cook the zucchini or summer squash and the ½ cup green onion in the water, covered, on 100% power (high) for 3 to 4 minutes or till the zucchini or summer squash is tender. Drain well. Cool slightly.

● Arrange the zucchini or summer squash slices and onion over the bottom and around the sides of an ungreased 9-inch pie plate, slightly overlapping the zucchini or squash slices on the sides of the pie plate.

● In the 1-quart casserole combine rice and milk. Cook, covered, on high for 2½ to 3½ minutes or till heated through, stirring once. Gradually stir rice mixture into eggs. Stir in the shredded cheese and salt. Carefully pour into the pie plate. Cook, uncovered, on 70% power (medium-high) for 6 to 9 minutes or till a knife inserted 2 inches from the center comes out clean, turning the dish once. The center will still appear wet.

● Sprinkle the tomato over the top. Let stand, uncovered, about 5 minutes or till the center is set. Sprinkle with additional green onion, if desired. Serve warm. Makes 8 servings.

Cheesy Corn Bake

No cheese crackers on hand? Try using crushed rich round or soda crackers.

1 tablespoon butter *or* margarine
¼ cup crushed bite-size cheese crackers
½ of a medium sweet red pepper *or* green pepper, cut into strips and halved
¼ cup sliced green onion
1 tablespoon butter *or* margarine
1 12-ounce can whole kernel corn, drained
1 cup shredded American cheese (4 ounces)
2 tablespoons milk

● In a custard cup cook 1 tablespoon butter or margarine, uncovered, on 100% power (high) for 30 to 40 seconds or till melted. Toss with the crushed crackers; set aside.

● In a 1-quart casserole combine the red or green pepper strips, onion, and 1 tablespoon butter or margarine. Cook, covered, on high for 1½ to 2½ minutes or till tender. Stir in the drained corn, shredded cheese, and milk. Cook, covered, on high for 2 to 4 minutes or till heated through, stirring twice. Sprinkle cracker mixture atop. Makes 4 servings.

Broccoli-Corn Bake

If you're using a 400- to 500-watt microwave, cook this on 70% power for 12 to 15 minutes.

 2 teaspoons butter *or*
　　margarine
 ¼ cup crushed whole wheat
　　crackers (6 crackers)
 1 cup frozen loose-pack cut
　　broccoli
 ¼ cup chopped onion
 1 tablespoon water
 1 beaten egg
 ⅓ cup crushed whole wheat
　　crackers (8 crackers)
 ¼ cup milk
 ¼ teaspoon dried thyme,
　　crushed
 ⅛ teaspoon pepper
 1 17-ounce can cream-style
　　corn

● In a 6-ounce custard cup cook the butter or margarine, uncovered, on 100% power (high) for 30 to 40 seconds or till melted. Toss together the melted butter and the ¼ cup crushed whole wheat crackers; set aside.

● In a medium bowl or a 1-quart casserole cook the broccoli and onion in water, covered, on high for 3 to 4 minutes or till the broccoli is crisp-tender. Drain. Spread the broccoli and onion in the bottom of a 6-cup ring mold.

● Stir together the egg, the ⅓ cup crushed crackers, milk, thyme, and pepper. Stir in the corn. Spread over the broccoli mixture. Cook, uncovered, on 70% power (medium-high) for 9 to 11 minutes or till the mixture is set and starts to pull away from the sides of the mold, turning the mold once. Sprinkle the crushed cracker mixture atop. Makes 4 servings.

Scalloped Tomatoes

Seasoned croutons streamline this old-time favorite.

 ½ cup chopped onion
 ¼ cup butter *or* margarine
 1¾ cups herb-seasoned stuffing
　　croutons
 1½ teaspoons sugar
 ⅛ teaspoon salt
 ⅛ teaspoon pepper
 4 medium tomatoes, peeled
　　and cut into wedges
　　Snipped parsley

● In a 1½-quart casserole combine the onion and butter or margarine. Cook, uncovered, on 100% power (high) for 2 to 4 minutes or till the onion is tender. Stir in the croutons, sugar, salt, and pepper.

● Gently stir in the tomatoes. Cook, uncovered, on high for 4 to 6 minutes or till heated through, stirring once. Stir, then sprinkle with snipped parsley. Makes 4 servings.

VEGETABLE SOUPS

Nothing tastes better on a cold day than hot soup. In this chapter you'll find all kinds of side-dish vegetable soups. Some are creamy and rich; others are made with well-seasoned broths. No matter what your favorite, add a sandwich and have a hearty lunch in minutes.

Microwave Oven Wattage

Most microwave ovens are either high wattage (600 to 700 watts) or low wattage (400 to 500 watts). We tested all of the recipes in this book in both types of ovens. Most of our recipes worked well in either— *except* for soups. We found a big difference between high- and low-wattage ovens in the cooking time of soups, because of the amount of liquid that the soups contain. Therefore, the time ranges for the recipes in this soups chapter are appropriate only for 600- to 700-watt ovens. If you have a lower-wattage microwave oven, lengthen the cooking time when you make the soup.

Chicken and Beef Broth Substitutes

When a recipe calls for chicken or beef broth, you can use stock you have on hand or one of the convenient commercial substitutes. Instant bouillon granules or cubes come in both beef and chicken flavors. Just mix these with water according to the package directions before using them as broth.

You can buy canned broth that may be used directly from the can. The cans usually contain 14½ ounces, which is about 1¾ cups of broth. Canned condensed beef and chicken broths are also available; dilute them with water before you use them as broth in a recipe.

Cheesy Potato-Beer Soup

This hearty side dish is a wonderful chill-chaser—perfect with a sandwich after sledding, skiing, or even snow shoveling.

3 medium potatoes, peeled and cut into ½-inch cubes (about 2 cups)
2 cups water
½ cup chopped onion
1 teaspoon instant chicken bouillon granules
¼ teaspoon salt
⅛ teaspoon pepper
Dash bottled hot pepper sauce
½ cup beer
2 tablespoons cornstarch
1 cup shredded American cheese (4 ounces)
Sliced green onion *or* chives (optional)

● In a 2-quart casserole combine the potatoes, water, onion, bouillon granules, salt, pepper, and hot pepper sauce. Cook, covered, on 100% power (high) for 9 to 11 minutes or till the potatoes are tender, stirring twice.

● Stir together the beer and cornstarch. Stir the beer mixture into the potato mixture. Cook, uncovered, on high for 1 to 2 minutes or till slightly thickened and bubbly, stirring every 30 seconds. Cook, uncovered, on high for 1 minute more. Stir in shredded cheese. Cook, uncovered, on high for 1 minute more or till heated through. Garnish with green onion or chives, if desired. Makes 4 servings.

Broccoli-Swiss Soup

Using process instead of natural cheese makes the soup smoother.

2 cups broccoli flowerets *or* one 10-ounce package frozen cut broccoli
1 cup chicken broth
½ cup finely chopped carrot
2 tablespoons finely chopped onion
3 tablespoons all-purpose flour
⅛ teaspoon pepper
1½ cups milk
1 cup shredded process Swiss cheese (4 ounces)

● If using fresh broccoli, in a 1½-quart casserole combine broccoli and 2 tablespoons *water*. Cook, covered, on 100% power (high) for 4 to 6 minutes or till the broccoli is crisp-tender. If using frozen broccoli, cook according to the package microwave directions. Drain the broccoli thoroughly.

● In the 1½-quart casserole combine ¼ *cup* of the chicken broth, the carrot, and onion. Cook, covered, on high for 3 to 5 minutes or till the carrot is crisp-tender. In a screw-top jar shake together the remaining broth, flour, and pepper.

● Stir the flour mixture and the milk into the carrot mixture. Cook, uncovered, on high for 7 to 9 minutes or till slightly thickened and bubbly, stirring each minute till the mixture starts to thicken, then stirring every 30 seconds. Cook, uncovered, on high for 1 minute more. Stir in the cheese and the broccoli. Cook, covered, on high for 1 minute more or till heated through. Makes 4 servings.

Vegetable Cheese Soup

Vegetable Cheese Soup

No cutting or chopping! Just use frozen mixed vegetables.

1 10-ounce package frozen mixed vegetables
½ cup water
1¼ cups milk
1 teaspoon instant chicken bouillon granules
½ teaspoon dry mustard
½ teaspoon dried oregano, crushed
½ teaspoon Worcestershire sauce
1½ cups shredded American cheese (6 ounces)
1 tablespoon all-purpose flour

● In a 1½-quart casserole combine the vegetables and water. Cook according to the package microwave directions. Stir in the milk, bouillon granules, dry mustard, oregano, and Worcestershire sauce. Cook, uncovered, on 100% power (high) for 3 to 5 minutes or just till bubbly around the edges.

● Toss together the cheese and flour; stir into hot vegetable mixture. Cook, uncovered, on high for 3 to 4 minutes or till slightly thickened and bubbly, stirring each minute till the mixture starts to thicken, then stirring every 30 seconds. Cook, uncovered, on high for 1 minute more. Makes 4 servings.

Cauliflower and Ham Chowder

Ham and cheese are natural go-togethers in this creamy chowder.

1 cup sliced cauliflower flowerets
½ cup water
¼ cup chopped onion
½ teaspoon instant chicken bouillon granules
1 cup light cream *or* milk
2 tablespoons all-purpose flour
½ teaspoon prepared mustard
½ cup diced fully cooked ham (2 ounces)
½ cup shredded American cheese (2 ounces)

● In a 1½-quart casserole combine cauliflower, water, onion, and bouillon granules. Cook, covered, on 100% power (high) for 6 to 8 minutes or till the cauliflower is tender, stirring once.

● Stir together the light cream or milk, flour, and mustard. Stir cream mixture and ham into the cauliflower mixture. Cook, uncovered, on high for 6 to 8 minutes or till thickened and bubbly, stirring each minute till the mixture starts to thicken, then stirring every 30 seconds. Cook, uncovered, on high for 1 minute more. Stir in cheese. Cook, uncovered, on high for 30 seconds more. Makes 3 servings.

Sherried Mushroom Soup

You'll find enoki mushrooms beside regular mushrooms in the produce section—look for their tiny caps and spaghetti-thin stems.

3 cups sliced fresh
　　mushrooms *or*
　　2 cups enoki mushrooms
½ cup chopped onion
½ cup finely chopped celery
2 tablespoons butter *or*
　　margarine
1 cup chicken broth
¼ teaspoon dried thyme,
　　crushed
⅛ teaspoon pepper
1 cup light cream
1 tablespoon cornstarch
3 tablespoons dry sherry

● In a 1½-quart casserole combine mushrooms, onion, celery, and butter or margarine. Cook, covered, on 100% power (high) for 5 to 7 minutes or till the mushrooms are tender, stirring twice. Stir in the broth, thyme, and pepper. Cook, covered, on high for 1 to 2 minutes or till heated through.

● Stir together the light cream and cornstarch. Stir into the hot mixture. Cook, uncovered, on high for 4 to 6 minutes or till the mixture is thickened and bubbly, stirring every minute. Cook, uncovered, on high for 30 seconds more. Stir in the sherry. Cook, covered, on high for 1 to 2 minutes or just till heated through. Makes 4 appetizer servings.

Creamy Celery and Rice Soup

1½ cups chicken broth
1 cup thinly sliced celery
¼ teaspoon finely shredded
　　lemon peel
　　Dash pepper
½ cup light cream *or* milk
1 tablespoon cornstarch
½ cup cooked rice
2 tablespoons sliced almonds,
　　toasted (optional)

● In a 1-quart casserole combine chicken broth, celery, lemon peel, and pepper. Cook, covered, on 100% power (high) for 9 to 11 minutes or till celery is tender, stirring once.

● Stir together light cream or milk and cornstarch. Stir cream mixture and rice into celery mixture. Cook, uncovered, on high for 2 to 3 minutes or till slightly thickened and bubbly, stirring each minute till the mixture starts to thicken, then stirring every 30 seconds. Cook, uncovered, on high for 1 minute more. If desired, sprinkle with almonds. Makes 3 servings.

Cauliflower and Broccoli Soup

Lightly seasoned with thyme, and oh, so creamy!

1 cup sliced cauliflower
  flowerets
1 cup broccoli flowerets
½ cup sliced green onion
½ cup chicken broth
¼ teaspoon dried thyme,
  crushed
  Dash pepper
1¼ cups chicken broth
¾ cup light cream *or* milk
¼ cup light cream *or* milk
2 tablespoons cornstarch

● In a 1½-quart casserole combine the cauliflower, broccoli, onion, ½ cup chicken broth, thyme, and pepper. Cook, covered, on 100% power (high) for 4 to 6 minutes or till the vegetables are crisp-tender, stirring once.

● Stir in the 1¼ cups broth and ¾ cup light cream or milk. Cook, covered, on high for 2 to 3 minutes or till heated through. Stir together the ¼ cup light cream or milk and cornstarch. Stir into the vegetable mixture.

● Cook, uncovered, on high for 4 to 6 minutes or till slightly thickened and bubbly, stirring each minute till the mixture starts to thicken, then stirring every 30 seconds. Cook, uncovered, on high for 1 minute more. Makes 3 servings.

Microwave French Onion Soup

Make this in less time than it takes to brown the onions for traditional French Onion Soup.

3 medium onions, thinly
  sliced and separated
  into rings
2 tablespoons butter *or*
  margarine
2 cups beef broth
1 teaspoon Worcestershire
  sauce
⅛ teaspoon pepper
  Plain croutons
  Shredded Swiss cheese

● In a 1-quart casserole cook the onions in butter or margarine, covered, on 100% power (high) for 6 to 8 minutes or till the onion is very tender, stirring once. Stir in the beef broth, Worcestershire sauce, and pepper. Cook, covered, on high for 4 to 6 minutes or till the mixture is heated through. Serve with croutons and cheese. Makes 3 servings.

Gingered Soup with Cellophane Noodles

Gingered Soup with Cellophane Noodles

Cellophane noodles? They get their name from their almost-clear appearance when cooked. You can find them at your supermarket with the Oriental foods.

1 ounce cellophane noodles
2 cups water
2 cups chicken broth
½ cup thinly sliced
    fresh mushrooms
1 medium carrot, thinly sliced
2 green onions, bias-sliced
    into 1-inch pieces
1 tablespoon soy sauce
1 teaspoon grated gingerroot
1 teaspoon lemon juice
1 clove garlic, minced
    Dash ground red pepper
½ cup fresh pea pods *or* ¼ of a
    6-ounce package frozen
    pea pods

● Break cellophane noodles into 2- to 3-inch pieces. Place in a bowl. In a 4-cup measure cook the water, uncovered, on 100% power (high) for 4 to 6 minutes or till boiling. Pour over the noodles. Let stand for 5 minutes. Drain.

● Meanwhile, in a 1½-quart casserole combine the chicken broth, mushrooms, carrot, green onions, soy sauce, gingerroot, lemon juice, garlic, and red pepper. Cook, covered, on high for 6 to 9 minutes or till the carrots are crisp-tender. Stir in cellophane noodles and pea pods. Cook, covered, on high for 2 to 3 minutes or till heated through and pea pods are crisp-tender. Makes 4 appetizer servings.

Fast Bean Soup

This toss-together soup starts with easy-to-use canned beans and tomatoes.

3 slices bacon, cut into 1-inch
    pieces
½ cup chopped onion
½ cup chopped celery
1 clove garlic, minced
1 16-ounce can tomatoes, cut
    up
1 15-ounce can great northern
    beans, drained
1¼ cups water
1 teaspoon instant chicken
    bouillon granules
½ teaspoon dried basil,
    crushed
¼ teaspoon ground sage
½ cup shredded cheddar
    cheese (2 ounces)

● Place the bacon in a 2-quart casserole. Cover with white paper towels. Cook on 100% power (high) for 3 to 5 minutes or till crisp-cooked. Use a slotted spoon to remove bacon, reserving drippings in the casserole. Set bacon aside.

● In the 2-quart casserole cook the onion, celery, and garlic in the reserved bacon drippings, covered, on high for 3 to 5 minutes or till the vegetables are tender. Drain off fat.

● Stir in the *undrained* tomatoes, drained beans, water, bouillon granules, basil, and sage. Cook, covered, on high for 7 to 9 minutes or till heated through. Stir in the bacon. Top with cheddar cheese. Makes 4 servings.

Tomato-Vegetable Soup

Tomato juice cocktail adds zip! For even more punch, try using hot-style tomato juice.

1 cup loose-pack frozen mixed
    vegetables
½ cup water
¼ cup quick-cooking rice
1½ cups tomato juice cocktail
1 7½-ounce can tomatoes, cut
    up
1 teaspoon sugar
½ teaspoon dried basil,
    crushed
½ teaspoon instant chicken
    bouillon granules

● In a 1½-quart casserole combine the vegetables, water, and rice. Cook according to the vegetable package microwave directions. Stir in the tomato juice cocktail, *undrained* tomatoes, sugar, basil, and bouillon granules. Cook, covered, on 100% power (high) for 3 to 4 minutes or till heated through, stirring once. Makes 4 servings.

Bacon and Tomato Soup

Tastes like a BLT sandwich—and you won't even miss the lettuce.

4 slices bacon, cut into 1-inch
    pieces
½ cup chopped onion
2 cloves garlic, minced
3 medium tomatoes, peeled,
    seeded, and chopped
⅓ cup tomato paste
2 tablespoons snipped parsley
½ teaspoon sugar
½ teaspoon dried thyme,
    crushed
⅛ to ¼ teaspoon pepper
1¾ cups chicken broth
    Dairy sour cream *or* plain
    yogurt

● Place bacon in a 1½-quart casserole. Cover with white paper towels. Cook on 100% power (high) for 3 to 5 minutes or till crisp-cooked. Drain bacon, reserving 1 tablespoon of the drippings. Set the bacon aside.

● In the 1½-quart casserole cook onion and garlic in the reserved bacon drippings, covered, on high for 1 to 2 minutes or till onion is tender. Stir in tomatoes, tomato paste, parsley, sugar, thyme, and pepper. Cook, covered, on high for 3 to 5 minutes or till tomatoes are very soft.

● Place tomato mixture in a blender container or food processor bowl. Cover and blend or process till the mixture is smooth. Return tomato mixture to the casserole. Stir in chicken broth. Cook, covered, on high for 3 to 5 minutes or till heated through, stirring once. Stir in bacon. Serve with sour cream or yogurt. Makes 4 servings.

STUFFED
VEGETABLES

When you want an out-of-the-ordinary vegetable, look to this chapter. You'll find a variety of vegetable shells stuffed with savory vegetable fillings. All of these side dishes are elegant presentations that just need a simple main dish to make a meal special enough for company.

Stuffed Vegetable Tips

Rearranging Food in the Microwave

In most microwave ovens, some parts of the oven cavity receive more microwave energy than others. That's why, when you're cooking large items such as whole vegetables, it's important to rearrange the food during cooking. For even cooking, move parts of the vegetables that are in the center of the dish to the outside. Also, change the position of the vegetables within the dish.

Preparing Vegetables for Stuffing

Nearly all vegetables need to be hollowed out if you want to stuff them. It's a cinch to scoop out soft vegetables, such as tomatoes—just use a spoon. But firmer vegetables may be more difficult. If you have trouble making a vegetable shell, try using an apple corer to get the cavity started. Then continue to carve the shell, using a spoon, melon baller, or grapefruit knife.

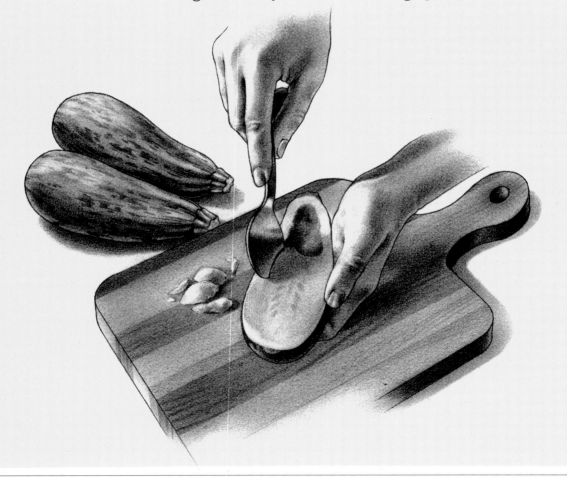

Salmon-Stuffed Mushroom Caps

For make-ahead appetizers, chill the stuffed mushrooms. Then cook, uncovered, on high for 4 to 6 minutes or till heated through. Pictured on page 7.

12 large fresh mushrooms (about 2 inches in diameter)
1 3¾-ounce can salmon, drained, flaked, and skin and bones removed
1 3-ounce package cream cheese, softened
1 tablespoon snipped parsley
1 teaspoon lemon juice
¼ teaspoon dried marjoram, crushed
Parsley sprigs (optional)

● Wash and dry the mushrooms. Remove the stems. Finely chop enough of the stems to make 1 cup. Set aside. Save any remaining stems for another use. In a 9-inch pie plate arrange the mushroom caps in a circle, stem side down. Cover with vented clear plastic wrap. Cook on 100% power (high) for 3 to 5 minutes or till almost tender, rearranging once. Drain.

● Meanwhile, stir together the reserved 1 cup mushroom stems, the salmon, cream cheese, parsley, lemon juice, and marjoram. Fill the mushroom caps with the salmon mixture. Arrange in a circle in the 9-inch pie plate. Cook, uncovered, on high for 3 to 5 minutes or till heated through, rearranging once. Garnish with parsley, if desired. Makes 4 appetizer servings.

Apple-Stuffed Onions

Onions, apple, and corn bread stuffing team up to make a fall harvest treat.

4 medium onions, peeled (about 1½ pounds)
2 tablespoons water
1 large apple, cored and chopped
1 clove garlic, minced
2 tablespoons butter *or* margarine
¾ cup corn bread stuffing mix
1 tablespoon snipped parsley
⅛ teaspoon pepper
¼ cup shredded cheddar cheese (1 ounce)

● Cut off the tops of the onions. Hollow out the onions, leaving a ¼-inch-thick shell. Save the insides of the onions for another use. Place the onions, cut side up, in an 8x8x2-inch baking dish. Add the water. Cover with vented clear plastic wrap. Cook on 100% power (high) for 5 to 7 minutes or till the onions are tender. Drain the onions by inverting them on paper towels.

● In a 1-quart casserole cook the apple and garlic in butter or margarine, covered, on high for 1 to 2 minutes or till the apple is tender. Stir in the corn bread stuffing mix, parsley, and pepper. Stir in the cheese. Spoon into the onions. Place in the 8x8x2-inch baking dish. Cover with vented clear plastic wrap. Cook on high for 1 to 2 minutes or till heated through, turning the dish once. Makes 4 servings.

Pasta 'n' Tomatoes

Stuffed to the brim with cheesy pasta!

1 cup tiny bow tie pasta
     (tripolini)
4 large fresh tomatoes
     (about 8 ounces each)
¼ cup sliced green onion
1 clove garlic, minced
1 tablespoon snipped fresh
     basil *or* 1 teaspoon dried
     basil, crushed
1 tablespoon butter *or*
     margarine
1 3-ounce package cream
     cheese, cubed
¼ cup shredded mozzarella,
     cheddar, *or* Swiss cheese
     (1 ounce)
¼ cup grated Parmesan cheese
⅛ teaspoon pepper
⅓ cup cubed fully cooked ham
¼ cup milk

● Cook pasta conventionally according to the package directions. Drain and keep warm. Meanwhile, cut a thin slice off the stem end of the tomatoes. Hollow out the tomatoes, leaving a ¼- to ½-inch-thick shell. Discard seeds. Chop the tomato insides and tops; set aside.

● In a 2-cup measure combine onion, garlic, basil, and butter or margarine. Cover with vented clear plastic wrap. Cook on 100% power (high) for 1 to 2 minutes or till the onion is tender. Stir together the warm pasta; cream cheese; mozzarella, cheddar, or Swiss cheese; Parmesan cheese; and pepper. Stir till the cheeses are slightly melted. Stir in the onion mixture, ham, and milk.

● Spoon about *½ cup* of the pasta mixture into *each* tomato. Spoon the remaining pasta mixture into an 8x8x2-inch baking dish. Sprinkle with the chopped tomato. Arrange the filled tomatoes in the dish atop the pasta mixture. Cover with vented clear plastic wrap. Cook on high for 6 to 8 minutes or till heated through. Let stand, covered, for 1 minute. Makes 4 servings.

Cheese-Filled Zucchini

Give this a try—hollow out zucchini with a melon baller. Pictured on page 6.

2 4- to 6-inch zucchini, halved
     lengthwise
2 tablespoons water
¼ cup chopped onion
1 clove garlic, minced
1 slightly beaten egg
¾ cup shredded Monterey
     Jack cheese (3 ounces)
½ cup corn bread stuffing mix
1 tablespoon butter *or*
     margarine, melted
1 tablespoon grated
     Parmesan cheese

● Scoop out the pulp of the zucchini halves, leaving a ¼-inch-thick shell. Chop the zucchini pulp; set aside. Place zucchini shells, cut side down, in an 8x8x2-inch baking dish. Add the water. Cover with vented clear plastic wrap. Cook on 100% power (high) for 2 to 4 minutes or till crisp-tender. Drain. Place, cut side up, in the 8x8x2-inch baking dish.

● In a 1-quart casserole combine the chopped pulp, onion, and garlic. Cook, covered, on high for 3 to 5 minutes or till tender. Drain in a colander, pressing out the excess liquid. In the 1-quart casserole stir together the egg, Monterey Jack cheese, stuffing mix, and butter or margarine. Stir in the zucchini pulp mixture. Spoon into the cooked zucchini shells. Sprinkle with Parmesan cheese. Cover with vented clear plastic wrap. Cook on high for 3 to 5 minutes or till the filling is heated through, rearranging once. Makes 4 servings.

Pasta 'n' Tomatoes

Spinach-Stuffed Artichokes

2 medium artichokes
(about 8 ounces each)
1 tablespoon lemon juice
¼ cup water
½ of a 10-ounce package
frozen chopped spinach
½ cup shredded carrot
¼ cup sliced green onion
2 tablespoons butter *or*
margarine
1 cup herb-seasoned stuffing
mix
1 beaten egg
¼ cup grated Parmesan cheese
⅛ teaspoon pepper

● Cut stems and loose outer leaves from artichokes. Cut off 1 inch from tops; snip off sharp leaf tips. Brush cut edges with lemon juice. Place the artichokes in an 8x4x2-inch loaf dish. Add the water. Cover with vented clear plastic wrap. Cook on 100% power (high) for 8 to 11 minutes or till a leaf pulls away easily, rearranging once. Drain. Let stand, uncovered, to cool.

● Meanwhile, cook spinach according to the package microwave directions. Drain in a colander, pressing out excess liquid. In a 1½-quart casserole cook carrot and onion in butter or margarine, covered, on high for 2 to 3 minutes or till tender. Stir in stuffing mix, egg, Parmesan, pepper, and cooked spinach.

● Remove center leaves and chokes from artichokes. Spread leaves slightly. Spoon spinach mixture into the centers of the artichokes and behind large leaves. Place in the 8x4x2-inch loaf dish. Cover with vented clear plastic wrap. Cook on high for 2 to 4 minutes or till heated through and bases of artichokes are tender. Makes 2 servings.

1 Trimming the artichokes
Start by using a sharp knife to remove the bottom stems so the artichokes will sit flat. Remove any loose outer leaves and cut off 1 inch of the tops of the artichokes. Then use kitchen shears, as shown in the picture, to snip off the sharp leaf tips. Be sure to brush lemon juice on all of the cut edges to keep them from turning brown.

2 Removing the chokes
After you've cooked the artichokes and they're cool enough for you to handle, use your fingers to pull out the center leaves. Then use a spoon to scoop out the fuzzy chokes. If you have trouble getting a choke out with the spoon, try loosening it with a grapefruit knife and then pulling it out with the spoon. Discard the chokes and the center leaves.

3 Stuffing the artichokes
Spread the leaves of each artichoke apart slightly. Using a spoon, loosely fill the center of the artichoke with stuffing. Then spoon a little bit of the additional stuffing (½ to 1 teaspoon) behind each large leaf, as shown.

Stuffed Turnips

For a milder-flavored stuffing, substitute leftover cooked lean beef for the ham.

4 medium turnips (6 to 8
ounces each)
¼ cup water
1 beaten egg
½ cup cubed fully cooked ham
½ cup shredded cheddar
cheese (2 ounces)
⅛ teaspoon pepper

● Peel off the outer skin of the turnips. Cut a thin slice off the bottoms so they sit flat. Place the turnips in an 8x8x2-inch baking dish. Add the water. Cover with vented clear plastic wrap. Cook on 100% power (high) for 14 to 16 minutes or till tender, rearranging the turnips once. Drain.

● Hollow out the centers of the turnips, leaving a ¼-inch-thick shell. Chop enough of the centers to make 1 cup. Save any remaining centers for another use. Stir together the egg, ham, cheese, and pepper. Stir in the 1 cup chopped turnip. Spoon the ham mixture into the turnip shells. Place in the 8x8x2-inch baking dish. Cover with vented clear plastic wrap. Cook on high for 2 to 4 minutes or till heated through. Makes 4 servings.

Sour Cream and Bacon Potatoes

No need to top these potatoes with butter—they're already packed with flavor.

4 slices bacon, cut into 1-inch
pieces
2 medium baking potatoes (5
to 6 ounces each)
½ cup dairy sour cream
1 tablespoon snipped chives
1 tablespoon snipped parsley
⅛ teaspoon pepper

● Place the bacon in a 1-quart casserole. Cover with white paper towels. Cook on 100% power (high) for 3 to 5 minutes or till crisp-cooked. Drain off fat. Set the bacon aside.

● Wash the potatoes. Prick skins. Cook the potatoes, uncovered, on high for 7 to 9 minutes or till tender. Halve the potatoes lengthwise. Scoop out the inside of each potato half, leaving a ¼-inch-thick shell. Mash the insides of the potatoes.

● Stir together the mashed potato, the bacon, sour cream, chives, parsley, and pepper. Pile mixture into the potato shells. Cook, uncovered, on high for 1 to 3 minutes or till heated through. Makes 4 servings.

MASHED
VEGETABLES

When you yearn for smooth and creamy vegetables, read through this chapter. You'll find the beloved mashed potatoes of your childhood, as well as sophisticated pureed vegetables that are just right for formal dinner parties. You can make all of them easily in your microwave oven.

Micro-Cooking Vegetable Pieces

Cut vegetables into pieces of uniform-size and shape before micro-cooking them. Larger pieces take longer to micro-cook than smaller ones. If pieces aren't uniform, some will be overcooked and others will be undercooked. But if you cut them all about the same size in a similar shape, they should micro-cook evenly.

Making Smooth Mashed Vegetables

For lump-free mashed vegetables, follow these handy suggestions.
● Cook the vegetables till they are *very* tender. They should be more than crisp-tender—they should be so tender that they fall apart when pierced with a fork.
● Some recipes indicate that vegetables can be mashed with either a mixer or a potato masher. A mixer will give a smoother consistency.
● Another alternative for mashing vegetables is to use a food mill. Pushing the vegetables through a food mill will yield a mashed vegetable that is as smooth as one made with an electric mixer.

Squash Sunflowers

Looks just like sunflowers!

4 large carrots, thinly sliced
    (2 cups)
3 tablespoons water
1 egg yolk
2 tablespoons butter
    or margarine
4 small pattypan squash
    (4 to 6 ounces each)
2 tablespoons water
2 tablespoons chopped
    pecans *or* sunflower seeds

● In a 1-quart casserole cook carrots in 3 tablespoons water, covered, on 100% power (high) for 8 to 10 minutes or till very tender, stirring once. *Do not drain.* In a blender container or food processor bowl combine carrots, cooking liquid, egg yolk, and butter or margarine. Cover and blend or process till smooth, stopping occasionally to push mixture into blades.

● If necessary, cut a thin slice from the stem end of each squash to allow the squash to stand upright. Turn blossom end up. Cut a thin slice from the blossom end. Using a small spoon scoop out squash center and seeds. Discard center and seeds.

● Sprinkle salt and pepper into each squash. Invert in a 12x7½x2-inch baking dish. Add 2 tablespoons water to the dish. Cover with vented clear plastic wrap. Cook on high for 6 to 8 minutes or till tender, rearranging the squash once. Drain. Turn squash over. Spoon some carrot mixture into each squash. Sprinkle pecans or sunflower seeds atop. In the 12x7½x2-inch baking dish cook, uncovered, on high for 1 to 2 minutes or till heated through. Makes 4 servings.

Basil Carrot Puree

Try piping cooled or chilled puree directly onto microwave-safe dinner plates. Then, before serving, pop each plate into the microwave and reheat for 30 seconds.

6 medium carrots, thinly
    sliced (3 cups)
⅓ cup water
3 to 4 tablespoons milk
⅛ teaspoon salt
⅛ teaspoon dried basil,
    crushed

● In a 1-quart casserole cook carrots in water, covered, on 100% power (high) for 12 to 15 minutes or till very tender, stirring twice. Drain. In a blender container or food processor bowl combine the carrots, milk, salt, and basil. Cover and blend or process till smooth.

● Place the mixture in a serving bowl. Cook, uncovered, on high for 1 to 2 minutes or till the mixture is heated through, stirring once. Makes 4 servings.

Pea Pâté in Pods

Eat these appetizers with your fingers—it's proper!

1½ cups loose-pack
    frozen peas
2 tablespoons water
4 teaspoons milk
¼ teaspoon dried chervil,
    crushed
    Dash pepper
4 ounces fresh pea pods
    (1⅓ cups)
2 tablespoons water

● In a 1-quart casserole cook the peas in 2 tablespoons water, covered, on 100% power (high) for 5 to 7 minutes or till very tender. Drain.

● In a blender container or food processor bowl combine the peas, milk, chervil, and pepper. Cover and blend or process till the pea skins are blended and the mixture is smooth.

● In the 1-quart casserole cook the pea pods in 2 tablespoons water, covered, on high for 1 to 2 minutes or till crisp-tender. Drain. Cool till easy to handle. Split the pea pods open lengthwise. Pipe or spoon the pea mixture into the pea pods. Loosely cover and chill. Makes 10 servings.

Lemon Potato Bake

Extra light and fluffy, with a hint of lemon.

4 medium potatoes, peeled
    and quartered
1 cup hot tap water
¾ cup milk
⅓ cup mayonnaise *or* salad
    dressing
1 egg yolk
½ teaspoon finely shredded
    lemon peel
1 teaspoon lemon juice
¼ teaspoon salt
⅛ teaspoon pepper
1 egg white
¼ cup fine dry bread crumbs
¼ cup shredded American
    cheese
2 tablespoons butter *or*
    margarine, melted

● In a 1½-quart casserole cook potatoes in water, covered, on 100% power (high) for 12 to 15 minutes or till very tender, stirring once. Drain. Mash potatoes with a potato masher or an electric mixer on low speed. Add milk, mayonnaise or salad dressing, egg yolk, lemon peel, lemon juice, salt, and pepper; beat till smooth.

● In a small bowl use a rotary beater to beat the egg white to stiff peaks. Fold the egg white into the potato mixture. Spoon into a 6-cup ring mold. Cook, uncovered, on 50% power (medium) for 10 to 12 minutes or till the mixture is just set, turning the dish 4 times.

● Toss together bread crumbs, cheese, and butter or margarine. Sprinkle atop the potato mixture. Cook, uncovered, on 100% power (high) for 30 seconds to 1 minute or till the cheese is melted. Let stand 5 minutes. Makes 6 to 8 servings.

1 Preparing fresh pea pods

To prepare fresh pea pods, remove their tips and strings. Use your fingers to pull off the tip of the pod without breaking the string. Then pull the string down the entire length of the pod. Remove the string from the pod and discard.

2 Filling the pea pods

First, fit a pastry bag with a medium-size star or round tip. Spoon the pea puree into the pastry bag and fold over the end of the bag. Hold the full bag against the palm of one hand. Use your other hand to hold a pea pod open.

To pipe the pea puree into the pea pod, place the tip of the pastry bag in one end of the pea pod. Squeeze the bag with your hand to force some puree out of the bag. At the same time, move the tip along the length of the open pea pod, as shown. Repeat with the remaining pea pods.

Cheesy Mashed Potatoes

Use a few fresh snipped chives and plain cream cheese if you can't find the cream cheese with chives in the dairy case.

4 medium potatoes, peeled and quartered
1 cup hot tap water
1 3-ounce package cream cheese with chives, cut up
2 tablespoons butter *or* margarine, cut up
¼ teaspoon salt
⅛ teaspoon pepper
⅓ to ½ cup milk

● In a 1½-quart casserole cook potatoes in water, covered, on 100% power (high) for 12 to 15 minutes or till very tender, stirring once. Drain.

● Mash potatoes with a potato masher or an electric mixer on low speed. Add cream cheese, butter or margarine, salt, and pepper. Gradually beat in enough milk to make potatoes light and fluffy. Spoon into the 1½-quart casserole. Cook, uncovered, on high for 2 to 4 minutes or till heated through, stirring once. Stir before serving. Makes 5 servings.

Fruited Mashed Sweet Potatoes

Great for Thanksgiving dinner.

½ cup mixed dried fruit bits
½ cup water
3 medium sweet potatoes, peeled and quartered
½ cup water
2 tablespoons butter *or* margarine, cut up
¼ teaspoon salt
½ to ⅔ cup milk

● In a 2-cup measure combine dried fruit and ½ cup water. Cook, covered, on 100% power (high) for 1½ to 2½ minutes or till boiling. Set aside.

● In a 1-quart casserole cook sweet potatoes in ½ cup water, covered, on high for 10 to 13 minutes or till very tender, stirring once. Drain both the potatoes and fruit.

● Mash potatoes with a potato masher or an electric mixer on low speed. Add fruit, butter or margarine, and salt. Gradually beat in enough milk to make potatoes light and fluffy. Spoon into the 1-quart casserole. Cook, uncovered, on high for 2 to 3 minutes or till heated through, stirring once. Makes 5 servings.

VEGETABLE COOKING CHART

VEGETABLE	METHOD	POWER LEVEL	COOKING TIME
▬ 1 1-pound acorn squash	▬ Wash the squash. Cut the squash in half, remove seeds, and prick the skin. Place squash halves, skin side up, and 2 tablespoons water in a 10x6x2-inch baking dish. Cover with vented clear plastic wrap. Micro-cook till tender, rearranging once. Drain.	100%	7 to 9 minutes
▬ 2 10-ounce artichokes	▬ Wash the artichokes; trim the stems. Cut off 1 inch from the tops and snip off sharp leaf tips. Brush cut edges with lemon juice. Place artichokes and 2 tablespoons water in a 2-quart casserole. Micro-cook, covered, till a leaf pulls out easily, rearranging once. Drain.	100%	7 to 10 minutes
▬ 1 pound asparagus spears	▬ Wash the asparagus and scrape off any scales. Break off the woody bases. Place asparagus spears and 2 tablespoons water in a 10x6x2-inch baking dish. Cover with vented clear plastic wrap. Micro-cook till crisp-tender, rearranging once. Drain.	100%	7 to 10 minutes
▬ 1 pound asparagus	▬ Wash asparagus and scrape off any scales. Break off woody bases. Cut into 1-inch pieces. Place asparagus and 2 tablespoons water in a 1½-quart casserole. Micro-cook, covered, till crisp-tender; stir once. Drain.	100%	7 to 9 minutes
▬ 1 pound green beans or wax beans	▬ Wash the beans. Cut into 1-inch pieces, if desired. Place beans and 2 tablespoons water in a 1½-quart casserole. Micro-cook, covered, till tender, stirring or rearranging once. Drain.	100%	16 to 19 minutes

VEGETABLE COOKING CHART

VEGETABLE	METHOD	POWER LEVEL	COOKING TIME
1 pound broccoli	Wash broccoli; remove outer leaves. Cut off tough parts of the stalks. Cut lengthwise into uniform spears, following the branching lines, or cut into ½-inch pieces. Place broccoli and 2 tablespoons water in a 10x6x2-inch baking dish. Cover with vented clear plastic wrap. Micro-cook till crisp-tender, stirring or rearranging once. Drain.	100%	6 to 9 minutes
½ pound brussels sprouts	Trim the stems. Remove any wilted outer leaves and wash. Cut any large sprouts in half to make all uniform size. Place brussels sprouts and 2 tablespoons water in a 1-quart casserole. Micro-cook, covered, till tender, stirring once. Drain.	100%	3 to 5 minutes
1 1½-pound butternut squash	Wash the squash. Cut the squash in half, remove seeds, and prick the skin. Place squash halves, skin side up, and 2 tablespoons water in a 10x6x2-inch baking dish. Cover with vented clear plastic wrap. Micro-cook till tender, rearranging once. Drain.	100%	10 to 13 minutes
1 pound carrots	Wash, trim, and peel carrots. Cut into ½-inch-thick slices. Place carrots and 2 tablespoons water in a 1½-quart casserole. Micro-cook, covered, till crisp-tender, stirring once. Drain.	100%	8 to 11 minutes
½ pound cauliflower	Wash cauliflower. Remove leaves and woody stem. Break cauliflower into flowerets. Place cauliflower and 2 tablespoons water in a 1½-quart casserole. Micro-cook, covered, till crisp-tender, stirring once. Drain.	100%	5 to 8 minutes

VEGETABLE	METHOD	POWER LEVEL	COOKING TIME
2 large stalks celery	Wash the celery. Cut into ½-inch-thick slices. Place the celery and 2 tablespoons water in a 1-quart casserole. Micro-cook, covered, till crisp-tender, stirring once. Drain.	100%	5 to 7 minutes
1 1¼-pound eggplant	Wash the eggplant. Cut off the cap. Peel, if desired, and cut into ¾-inch cubes. Place eggplant and 2 tablespoons water in a 2-quart casserole. Micro-cook, covered, till tender, stirring once. Drain.	100%	6 to 9 minutes
½ pound mushrooms	Wash the mushrooms. Cut into ¼-inch-thick slices. Place mushrooms and 2 tablespoons water in a 1-quart casserole. Micro-cook, covered, till tender, stirring once. Drain.	100%	2½ to 3½ minutes
1 medium onion	Peel and chop onion. Place onion and 2 tablespoons water in a 2-cup measure. Cover with vented clear plastic wrap. Micro-cook till tender. Drain.	100%	2 to 3 minutes
½ pound parsnips	Wash, trim, and peel parsnips. Cut into ¼-inch-thick slices. Place parsnips and 2 tablespoons water in a 1-quart casserole. Micro-cook, covered, till crisp-tender, stirring once. Drain.	100%	4 to 6 minutes
2 pounds shelled peas	Place peas and 2 tablespoons water in a 1-quart casserole. Micro-cook, covered, till tender, stirring once. Drain.	100%	6 to 8 minutes

VEGETABLE COOKING CHART

VEGETABLE	METHOD	POWER LEVEL	COOKING TIME
6 ounces pea pods	Remove tips and strings. Place pods and 2 tablespoons water in a 1-quart casserole. Micro-cook, covered, till crisp-tender; stir once. Drain.	100%	3 to 5 minutes
1 medium sweet red, yellow, or green pepper	Wash pepper. Remove seeds and chop. Place pepper and 2 tablespoons water in a 1-quart casserole. Micro-cook, covered, till crisp-tender, stirring once. Drain.	100%	3 to 5 minutes
2 6- to 8-ounce baking potatoes	Wash potatoes and prick skins in several places. Micro-cook, uncovered, till tender, rearranging once.	100%	8 to 10 minutes
4 6- to 8-ounce baking potatoes	Wash potatoes and prick skins in several places. Micro-cook, uncovered, till tender, rearranging once.	100%	14 to 17 minutes
1 pound rutabaga	Wash and peel rutabaga. Cut into ½-inch cubes. Place rutabaga and 2 tablespoons water in a 2-quart casserole. Micro-cook, covered, till tender, stirring three times. Drain.	100%	12 to 16 minutes
1 pound spinach	Wash spinach. Remove large center vein. Place spinach and 2 tablespoons water in a 3-quart casserole. Micro-cook, covered, till tender, stirring once. Drain.	100%	7 to 9 minutes
1 pound zucchini	Wash zucchini and cut into ¼-inch-thick slices. Place zucchini and 2 tablespoons water in a 1½-quart casserole. Micro-cook, covered, till tender, stirring two times. Drain.	100%	7 to 9 minutes

Index

A–B

Apple-Stuffed Onions, 63
Artichokes
  Buymanship, 11
  Cooking, 75
  Spinach-Stuffed
    Artichokes, 66
Asparagus
  Asparagus with Lemon
    Sauce, 38
  Buymanship, 11
  Cooking, 75
Baby Carrots in Sauterne, 34
Bacon and Tomato Soup, 60
Basil Carrot Puree, 71
Beans
  Buymanship, 12
  Cooking, 75
  Easy Green Bean
    Casserole, 42
  Fast Baked Beans, 46
  Fast Bean Soup, 59
  Hot Spinach-Bean Salad, 28
  Molasses Beans, 46
  Wax Beans with
    Tomatoes, 37
Beets, Buymanship, 12
Beets, Orange, 34
Broccoli
  Broccoli-Corn Bake, 50
  Broccoli-Swiss Soup, 53
  Buymanship, 13
  Cauliflower and Broccoli
    Soup, 57
  Cooking, 76
  Creamy Broccoli and Rice, 41
  Orange-Buttered Broccoli, 31
  Sesame Cauliflower and
    Broccoli, 29
Brussels Sprouts
  Brussels Sprouts
    Parmesan, 32
  Buymanship, 13
  Cooking, 76

C–F

Cabbage, Buymanship, 14
Candied Acorn Squash, 34
Carrots
  Baby Carrots in Sauterne, 34
  Basil Carrot Puree, 71

Carrots *(continued)*
  Buymanship, 14
  Carrots and Pea Pods, 29
  Cooking, 76
  Gingered Soup with
    Cellophane Noodles, 59
  Harvest Vegetable Bake, 45
  Squash Sunflowers, 71
Casseroles, 41-50
Cauliflower
  Buymanship, 15
  Cauliflower and Broccoli
    Soup, 57
  Cauliflower and Ham
    Chowder, 55
  Cooking, 76
  Garlic-Buttered
    Cauliflower, 29
  Sesame Cauliflower and
    Broccoli, 29
Celeriac, Buymanship, 15
Celeriac Alfredo, 37
Celery
  Buymanship, 15
  Celery Amandine, 33
  Cooking, 77
  Creamy Celery and Rice
    Soup, 56
Cheese-Filled Zucchini, 64
Cheesy Corn Bake, 49
Cheesy Mashed Potatoes, 74
Cheesy Potato Bake, 41
Cheesy Potato-Beer Soup, 53
Corn
  Broccoli-Corn Bake, 50
  Buymanship, 16
  Cheesy Corn Bake, 49
  Corn-on-the-Cob, 32
  Squash-Corn Casserole, 47
Creamy Broccoli and Rice, 41
Creamy Celery and Rice
  Soup, 56
Cumin Peppers and Onion, 26
Custard-in-Squash Pie, 49
Easy Green Bean Casserole, 42
Easy Vegetable-Rice Bake, 46

Eggplant
  Buymanship, 16
  Cooking, 77
  Eggplant and Tomato, 25
  Microwave Eggplant
    Parmigiana, 42
Fast Baked Beans, 46
Fast Bean Soup, 59
Fruited Mashed Sweet Potatoes,
  74

G–O

Garlic-Buttered Cauliflower, 29
German-Style Potato and
  Spinach Salad, 31
Gingered Soup with Cellophane
  Noodles, 59
Green Onions and Bacon, 25
Harvest Vegetable Bake, 45
Hot Spinach-Bean Salad, 28
Kohlrabi, Buymanship, 17
Lemon Potato Bake, 72
Mashed Vegetables, 71–74
Microwave Eggplant
  Parmigiana, 42
Microwave French Onion
  Soup, 57
Molasses Beans, 46
Mushrooms
  Buymanship, 17
  Cooking, 77
  Gingered Soup with
    Cellophane Noodles, 59
  Oriental Vegetables, 38
  Salmon-Stuffed Mushroom
    Caps, 63
  Savory Mushrooms, 25
  Sherried Mushroom Soup, 56
Okra, Buymanship, 18
Onions
  Apple-Stuffed Onions, 63
  Buymanship, 18
  Cooking, 77
  Cumin Peppers and
    Onion, 26
  Green Onions and Bacon, 25
  Microwave French Onion
    Soup, 57
  Oriental Vegetables, 38
Orange Beets, 34
Orange-Buttered Broccoli, 31
Oriental Vegetables, 38

P–R

Parmesan-Topped Tomato
    Slices, 26
Parsnips, Buymanship, 19
Parsnips, Cooking, 77
Pasta 'n' Tomatoes, 64
Peas
    Buymanship, 19
    Carrots and Pea Pods, 29
    Cooking, 77, 78
    Gingered Soup with
        Cellophane Noodles, 59
    Oriental Vegetables, 38
    Pea Pâté in Pods, 72
    Peas and Walnuts, 26
Peppers
    Buymanship, 20
    Cooking, 78
    Cumin Peppers and
        Onion, 26
    Garlic-Buttered
        Cauliflower, 29
Potatoes
    Buymanship, 20
    Cheesy Mashed Potatoes, 74
    Cheesy Potato Bake, 41
    Cheesy Potato-Beer Soup, 53
    Cooking, 78
    German-Style Potato and
        Spinach Salad, 31
    Lemon Potato Bake, 72
    Sour Cream and Bacon
        Potatoes, 68
Rutabagas
    Buymanship, 22
    Cooking, 78
    Harvest Vegetable Bake, 45

S–Z

Salad, German-Style Potato and
    Spinach, 31
Salad, Hot Spinach-Bean, 28
Salmon-Stuffed Mushroom
    Caps, 63
Savory Mushrooms, 25
Scalloped Tomatoes, 50
Sesame Cauliflower and
    Broccoli, 29

Sherried Mushroom Soup, 56
Soups, 53–60
Sour Cream and Bacon
    Potatoes, 68
Spicy Squash Bake, 45
Spinach
    Buymanship, 21
    Cooking, 78
    German-Style Potato and
        Spinach Salad, 31
    Hot Spinach-Bean Salad, 28
    Spinach-Stuffed
        Artichokes, 66
Squash
    Buymanship, 21
    Candied Acorn Squash, 34
    Cooking, 75, 76, 78
    Custard-in-Squash Pie, 49
    Spicy Squash Bake, 45
    Squash-Corn Casserole, 47
    Squash Sunflowers, 71
Steamed Vegetables, 25–38
Stuffed Turnips, 68
Stuffed Vegetables, 63–68
Sweet Potatoes
    Buymanship, 22
    Fruited Mashed Sweet
        Potatoes, 74
    Harvest Vegetable Bake, 45
Tomatoes
    Bacon and Tomato Soup, 60
    Buymanship, 22
    Eggplant and Tomato, 25
    Fast Bean Soup, 59
    Microwave Eggplant
        Parmigiana, 42
    Parmesan-Topped Tomato
        Slices, 26
    Pasta 'n' Tomatoes, 64
    Scalloped Tomatoes, 50
    Tomato-Vegetable Soup, 60
    Wax Beans with
        Tomatoes, 37
Turnips, Buymanship, 22
Turnips, Stuffed, 68
Vegetables
    Easy Vegetable-Rice Bake, 46
    Tomato-Vegetable Soup, 60
    Vegetable Cheese Soup, 55
    Vegetable Rice Soup, 60
Wax Beans with Tomatoes, 37
Zucchini, Cheese-Filled, 64
Zucchini with Walnuts, 32

Tips

Baking Dishes and
    Casseroles, 40
Chicken and Beef Broth
    Substitutes, 52
Making Smooth Mashed
    Vegetables, 70
Micro-Cooking Vegetable
    Pieces, 70
Microwave Oven Wattage, 52
Preparing Vegetables for
    Stuffing, 62
Rearranging Food in the
    Microwave, 62
Simple Casserole
    Garnishes, 40
Toasting Nuts in Your
    Microwave Oven, 24
What is Crisp-Tender?, 24

Are you always on the lookout for more microwave recipes? Then, *Better Homes and Gardens®* has the books you need. When you're cooking for just yourself, give *Microwave Cooking for One or Two* a try. Are the kids fascinated by the microwave oven? Then have them cook dinner using *Microwave Cooking for Kids.* Or, if you're just starting out with microwave cooking, *Microwave Recipes Made Easy* will help with the basics. You can count on these and many other microwave cookbooks from *Better Homes and Gardens®* for excellent results every time.